BURN YOUR SHIPS

Burn Your Ships: *An Unapologetic Manual for Leaving Empty Religion for a Life Marked by Revival*

Copyright © 2023 Kelly Lohrke

All rights reserved. No part of this publication may be reproduced in a retrieval system, or transmitted in any form or by any means—electronic, mechanical, photocopying, recording, or otherwise—without the prior written permission of the publisher.

Scripture taken from the New King James Version®. Copyright © 1982 by Thomas Nelson. Used by permission. All rights reserved. | All Scripture quotations are taken from THE MESSAGE, copyright © 1993, 2002, 2018 by Eugene H. Peterson. Used by permission of NavPress, represented by Tyndale House Publishers. All rights reserved. | Scripture quotations marked TPT are from The Passion Translation®. Copyright © 2017, 2018 by Passion & Fire Ministries, Inc. Used by permission. All rights reserved. ThePassionTranslation.com.| Scripture quotations marked (CEV) are from the Contemporary English Version Copyright © 1991, 1992, 1995 by American Bible Society. Used by Permission.| Scripture quotations marked (NLT) are taken from the Holy Bible, New Living Translation, copyright ©1996, 2004, 2015 by Tyndale House Foundation. Used by permission of Tyndale House Publishers, Carol Stream, Illinois 60188. All rights reserved. | Scripture quotations from The Authorized (King James) Version. Rights in the Authorized Version in the United Kingdom are vested in the Crown. Reproduced by permission of the Crown's patentee, Cambridge University Press. | Scripture quotations marked (AMPC) taken from the Amplified® Bible (AMPC), Copyright © 1954, 1958, 1962, 1964, 1965, 1987 by The Lockman Foundation. Used by permission. lockman.org. | Scripture quotations marked (PARA) are paraphrased versions of the original passage by the author, while maintaining fidelity to the original Hebrew, Greek, and Aramaic texts.

This manuscript has undergone viable editorial work and proofreading, yet human limitations may have resulted in minor grammatical or syntax-related errors remaining in the finished book. The understanding of the reader is requested in these cases. While precaution has been taken in the preparation of this book, the publisher and author assume no responsibility for errors or omissions, or for damages resulting from the use of the information contained herein.

This book is set in the typeface *Athelas* designed by Veronika Burian and Jose Scaglione.

Hardcover ISBN: 978-1-088009-11-6
Paperback ISBN: 978-1-955546-34-8

A Publication of *Tall Pine Books*
119 E Center Street, Suite B4A | Warsaw, Indiana 46580
www.tallpinebooks.com

| 1 23 23 20 16 02 |

Published in the United States of America

BURN YOUR SHIPS

AN UNAPOLOGETIC MANUAL FOR LEAVING EMPTY RELIGION FOR A LIFE MARKED BY REVIVAL

KELLY LOHRKE

"Discipleship is the lost assignment of the church today. The church has focused on making services, ministries, and conferences all while losing sight of making disciples. This is our Great Commission. This is the assignment of the church and the dedicated Christ follower. I admire Pastor Kelly Lohrke's passion for discipleship. Kelly is an evangelist at heart. I've lost count of the times where he has shared the Gospel and love of Jesus with strangers in public. Every time I'm with him a random person comes up to him and testifies of how they gave their life to the Lord and put their faith in Jesus at a service he ministered at. As Kelly has committed his life to reach the lost, he has also given his life to disciple the found. I honor this man and celebrate the wisdom of God in him from a life dedicated to discipleship."

Pastor Landon Schott
Lead Pastor of *Mercy Culture Church*

"Pastor Kelly was every bit as raw and unfiltered with me about Jesus as he is in this book. In my toughest trial, he told me everything I needed to hear, but didn't want to hear. In my opinion, every one of his sermons he should published."

Pastor Gerardo Mejia,
Formerly, "Rico Suave" and Pastor of *House of Grace*

"Evangelism, Discipleship, Church Planting. Core values in Cure Churches led by Apostle Kelly Lohrke. Souls. Souls. Souls are the determined, hardcore, motivation and cry of this passionate book and its Author. For 28 years I have known Kelly and Esther and never once have they wavered from these words in the book: 'Jesus is calling us to radical love and obedience in the area of evangelism and influence.' You will be stirred again to serve your world as Jesus did the entire world in reading this book. He writes as he preaches: no holds barred!"

IRVIN RUTHERFORD
Founder and Leader, *Global Ministry Teams*

"Pastor Kelly Lohrke has been a spiritual father for more than half of my life. And in that time I've had the opportunity to observe his life up close and personal—he is most definitely the real deal. With a heart of integrity and an unashamed approach to evangelism and discipleship, his message is (and has always been) clear: Go all in for Jesus! This book embodies that message. Don't just read it, do it!"

J. ZACK WILLIAMSON
Lead Pastor, *The Cure Church* Chicago

"Over the last 52 years, I've had the great honor of standing in places where I knew pastors had made an investment in their congregation and their spiritual maturity. But I have never been anywhere quite like The Cure Church. Pastor Kelly Lohrke is not only a great discipleship teacher, he models every word of his instruction. I am in awe of the focus, the quality of life, and the depth of Bible knowledge, that I see, hear, and experience in Pastor Lohrke's congregation. This book is not written from the perspective of a researcher, who is simply putting good ideas end to end until a book is done. This book is the glorious result of a life that has been lived so remarkably well, that others have and will continue to emulated the principles and truths found here in these pages. Enjoy this read and be forever changed."

DENNY DURON
Pastor, *Shreveport Community Church*

CONTENTS

1. Common Misconceptions 1
2. Uncommon Prayer 15
3. Radical Worship 25
4. Insatiable Hunger 43
5. Hardcore Love 61
6. Remaining Teachable 77
7. Tangible Impartation 95
8. Sanctified Violence 111
9. True Treasure 123
10. Unmatched Adventure 141

Afterword: An Exhortation To Men 151
Meet the Author 167

CHAPTER ONE

COMMON MISCONCEPTIONS

WHEN THEY HIT the coast, they pulled their boats onto the land. They had sailed a long way but still had a grueling, bloody road ahead. The men likely thought they would immediately rush forward, inland to fight and conquer the Aztec empire in Mexico. But instead, they heard a unique order from their Spanish captain, Hernán Cortés. It was simple but weighty.

"Burn the ships."

What!? It was unheard of. It was a challenge. It was a statement. It was *necessary*. The command was a loud and clear declaration that they would either conquer or die, but retreat was not going to be an option. The men burned their plan B and forged ahead, knowing they would either win or give their lives for the cause. They would not look over their shoulder nor be tempted by the allure of retreat and defeat. Within two years, Cortés and his men had conquered the Aztec empire. Had their backup plan been waiting for them on the water's edge, they may have cut and run.

One thousand five hundred years before Cortés and his men torched their boats, Jesus Christ released a phrase with similar sentiments: "No man, having put his hand to the plow, and looking back, is fit for the kingdom of God" (Luke 9:62 NKJV). Discipleship is not for the faint of heart. Jesus is not one god among many. He is not a menu item to be compared with other options. He is the one true living God, and following after Him means burning your alternatives and never looking back.

Here's the nitty gritty: if you are unsure, you are unfit. Jesus made it clear; those who are fit for the kingdom have just one direction, and that is *forward*. Retreat is defeat. The entire drift of this book is to define discipleship and call you, the reader, into it. But first things first. Before we describe what discipleship *is,* we need to understand what it *is not*. There are a number of misconceptions surrounding the subject, and right out of the gate, I want to dismantle those carefully and biblically.

Misconception #1: No Second Chances

Some believe there are no second chances with the call of God. Many feel that after you've taken your hand off the plow to look back, you have no ability to put your hand back on the plow and pick up where you left off. Biblically, this is simply not the case.

To set this up, let's take a glimpse at the life of Peter.

For over three years, Peter was a faithful disciple. He was a sponge absorbing from Jesus and pouring out onto others. He witnessed Christ perform amazing miracles, heard Him preach and teach about the kingdom of God, and saw the masses come and go. It was an unmatched three-year degree.

However, when Jesus was arrested at the Garden of Gethsemane, Peter lost his courage and driving passion. He had once been so close to Jesus but now followed at a distance. In fact, the scripture says, "And those who had laid hold of Jesus led Him away to Caiaphas the high priest, where the scribes and the elders were assembled. But Peter followed Him at a distance" (Matthew 26:57-58 NKJV).

Peter was then confronted about his relationship with Jesus by curious bystanders. Of course, he strongly denied even knowing Him, not just once, but three times. At the crowing of the rooster, he was reminded of Jesus' words, "...before the rooster crows, you will deny Me three times" (Matthew 26:34 NKJV).

It was tragic. Peter had looked back. He had taken his hand off the plow. He was slipping back into the boat to retreat. Fear won the day while faith took a back seat. Peter then withdrew from the crowd and wept bitter tears, broken at his own capacity to betray His friend and master. Yet the story was not over. After His resurrection, Jesus appeared to Peter by the sea and initiated conversation. It went like this:

So when they had eaten breakfast, Jesus said to

Simon Peter, "Simon, son of Jonah, do you love Me more than these?" He said to Him, "Yes, Lord; You know that I love You." He said to him, "Feed My lambs." He said to him again a second time, "Simon, son of Jonah, do you love Me?" He said to Him, "Yes, Lord; You know that I love You." He said to him, "Tend My sheep." He said to him the third time, "Simon, son of Jonah, do you love Me?" Peter was grieved because He said to him the third time, "Do you love Me?" And he said to Him, "Lord, You know all things; You know that I love You." Jesus said to him, "Feed My sheep. Most assuredly, I say to you, when you were younger, you girded yourself and walked where you wished; but when you are old, you will stretch out your hands, and another will gird you and carry you where you do not wish." This He spoke, signifying by what death he would glorify God. And when He had spoken this, He said to him, "Follow Me." (John 21:15-19 NKJV)

Peter's original call to be a disciple was restored in that encounter with Jesus. In fact, it was by that very body of water that Jesus had told him, "Follow Me," to begin with. From that point on, Peter became the disciple that he was meant to be and never looked back. Not only was a second chance given, but in Peter's life and in our lives, second, third, fourth, fifths and far beyond are given.

Misconception #2: My Faith Has Its Own Compartment

As humans, we love to compartmentalize our lives. We divide up our schedules and attention between spiritual stuff and work stuff, between work stuff and family stuff, and between family stuff and no stuff. The problem is, your faith does not belong in a compartment. Your faith, or lack thereof, bleeds into every area of your life. In the same way that Peter's devotion to Jesus had an all-encompassing effect on his destiny, your devotion will do the same for you.

Discipleship is a calling, not a compartment. In fact, 77 times in just the four gospels, the term *call* is used in conjunction with discipleship. While being a faithful church member is important, the true gospel speaks of discipleship.

Many of us see our vocations as our main calling. We may declare that we are called to be a lawyer, a biker, an architect, or a singer for Jesus. Yet I do not find this in the Bible. The New Testament church is commissioned, or called, to be and to make disciples. Now, the place you may do that might be in a law office or on the showroom floor of a dealership. But at the end of the day, the overarching call is to be and to make disciples. To pull this off, faith cannot fit into a Sunday box. In fact, our job is to make disciples, and in order to make disciples, you have to be one. You cannot disciple in other people what you have not first established in yourself. Yet people do this with discipleship all the time, choosing a "do as I say, not as I do" philosophy instead.

The fact is, discipleship is far more profound than any kind of book that you can read or any kind of class you can take. It is more than just going to Bible college or checking your church attendance box on Sunday. It's supernatural. God does a spiritual work in the hearts of men and women to transform them. More than head knowledge, this is spiritual training where we receive impartation and character formation. There are many types of natural training to gain knowledge and skills, but spiritual training is an internal work within the heart. No matter the vocation or education, God's purpose for us all is bigger and of greater importance. Let it be unleashed into every area.

Misconception #3: Only Some are Called to Great Devotion.

There is a clergy versus laity mentality floating around out there. The Roman Catholic church operates with this sort of priest and laity position where the papacy exists high up and holy, whereas the laity exists down low with lesser devotion. Most Catholics believe the priest is exclusively the holy one and is expected to live a holy life as a result. He is the one that is supposed to be devoted and consecrated to God. He is expected to dress and act a certain way and is also forbidden from marrying. Invariably this kind of thinking has leaked into the church as a whole.

The preacher is the one that is supposed to live a holy life, but everyone else is just another sinner in the pew. Religiosity promotes something different. The fact is, *all* believers are called to wholehearted devotion, not just some.

It's not as though the preacher and ministry staff are on the court while the church members are all in the bleachers. We are all in the game.

As the people of God, we are not spectators. We are not called to show up and punch a ticket while living like the world for the rest of the week. That is not New Testament Christianity. Jesus asked Peter three times if he loved Him and each time instructed Peter to care for His people. Essentially Jesus was telling Peter not to just talk the talk, but to walk the walk. If Peter really was devoted to Jesus, he would have a heart for the sheep and lambs, period. It was where rubber met the road. In order to demonstrate his love for God, Peter was to feed and tend to Jesus' sheep and lambs.

Like Peter, our love for God is manifested when we reach out to somebody else, especially the lost. But this is not merely a preacher's job. Christians are not meant to sit back and let "the called ones" live out God's will. Why? Because we are *all* called.

Misconception #4: We Write the Rules

The word disciple means "one who learns." This means that we learn and apply the standards of God, not that we create them ourselves. Too many people want God but they only want God on their own terms. This is not discipleship; this is rebellion. It's true, many people do indeed feel that they can be a Christian in name only and live as they please otherwise. They might not say it out loud, but their behavior snitches on their hearts.

In the verses we read prior, Jesus told Peter that when he was young in the Lord, he came and went as he pleased but he was not going to be able to do that as he matured. He even addressed the reality that the disciples would die for Him, and they were still willing to follow. Today, many say they will die for Jesus, but my challenge to them is, why don't you try to *live* for Him now?

The fact is, it's easy to say you would take a bullet for the cause of Christ. But will you clean toilets for the cause of Christ? We often honor and romanticize martyrdom. But in reality, there is a not-so-glorious, pedestrian, normal, day-in and day-out devotion to serving that precedes martyrdom.

Living for Jesus demands that He is not just Savior but Lord. There comes a time when we all must realize that our lives are truly not our own. We are not just yielding to a one-time rescue mission from Jesus as He snatches us out of hell. We are yielding to a full-time marriage to the Bridegroom of Heaven.

Misconception #5: It Needs to Be Fair

Finally, there is a myth that all things must be *fair* in the kingdom. God is not so much concerned about what is fair but what is righteous. Shortly after Peter was restored back to his calling, he received a gigantic newsflash. Jesus minced no words telling Peter that he would one day be killed for his faith (see John 21:18-19).

Instead of letting the gravity of this word sink in, Peter immediately played the comparison game. Fairness was probably on his mind. He turns around and sees John and asks, "Hey Jesus, what about this guy?" (John 21:21 PARA). His concern was not that he would be killed for his faith but if John would also be part of that crew.

Jesus gave Peter a short and sweet correction: "If I will that he remain till I come, what is that to you? You follow Me" (John 21:22 NKJV). In other words, you cannot go about the work of the Father if you are too busy prying into the work of your brother.

This happens in church. Pastors assign various tasks to different people. Invariably some guy with a bad attitude will demand to know why he has to do a certain task that no one else does. Jesus's response to Peter made it clear that if He gave John a walk on easy street, would Peter still follow Him? If you get the short end of the stick, or an unfair plight, will you still remain devoted to Jesus, or will you cave to comparison?

There are those who are more committed and will be given more responsibility, while others are given less. A disciple should resist the temptation to compare themselves with others. John was one of the 12 who did not die from martyrdom. But he didn't have it easy; he was thrown in a vat of boiling oil and supernaturally survived. He was later exiled to the island of Patmos where he wrote the book of Revelation and died of natural causes. Peter, however, died by upside-down crucifixion. Each man lived and died doing the will of God for their life. At the end of the day, this is what matters. Not who had it better or worse.

Defining Hardcore

The disciples of Christ followed Him closely with a fervency and zeal that can only be described as hardcore. This is what God is after because as we live out our faith this way, we are able to reach others too. Not only that, but we will be able to withstand what is to come on the earth. The call that is going out now is a call to hardcore discipleship.

After some study of the word hardcore, I would define it this way. Hardcore (adjective): *extremely resistant, inflexible in purpose, intensely loyal, steadfast, dedicated, persistent, strong, tough, and completely faithful.*

This is the biblical instruction to you and I also. Paul said, "Therefore, my beloved brethren, be steadfast, immovable, always abounding in the work of the Lord, knowing that your labor is not in vain in the Lord" (1 Corinthians 15:58 NKJV). It's super simple. Paul is highlighting the qualities that define hardcore disciples. For believers, this hardcore passion comes when we truly follow Jesus with our whole hearts. Twelve men left everything to follow Jesus and not only were their lives changed, they also turned the world upside down. Disciples are changed people, and changed people change the world.

The world displays hardcore living differently than we do. A certain drive to excel, succeed or win exists in every area of life and profession. Boxers or MMA fighters have a killer instinct. They will fight, sell out, train, and allow themselves to be beaten up in order to hone their ability. Businessmen achieve success by climbing the corporate ladder. Gung-ho soldiers are driven to be the best of the best, able to carry out the most intense of missions.

Isn't it amazing how crazy we can get for the world and still become such pushovers for God? Hardcore passion is a quality that anyone who desires to be great must have, especially when it comes to the kingdom of God.

Without a doubt, hardcore discipleship means letting Jesus lead. Letting Jesus lead means you hop out of the driver's seat. Jesus made this clear when He said, *"Anyone who intends to come with me has to let Me lead"* (Matthew 16:24-26 MSG). This passage is not just a good slogan for a t-shirt or a phrase to repeat. A disciple lets God lead in every area, practically and functionally. Most of us do not like to take orders. We pride ourselves in saying we are submissive—*but are we really?* Yes, we are good imitators of Christ and we do so frequently, but Jesus is asking much more than just imitating an outward appearance or behavior. He goes on:

> You are not in the driver's seat, I am. Don't run from suffering; embrace it. Follow me and I'll show you how. Self-help is no help at all. Self-sacrifice is the way, my way, to finding yourself, your true self. What kind of deal is it to get everything you want but lose yourself? What could you ever trade your soul for? (Matthew 16:24-26 MSG)

This is the very essence of discipleship. Jesus was showing His disciples the way to really live life. It is the opposite of what this world teaches. We have been taught to climb the ladder of success, compromise, and put ourselves first. But Jesus entered the picture and He flipped it all around. Self-sacrifice and trusting Him to lead is the new way to live.

We may say that we trust Jesus, but that trust gets tested. We all have a combination of strong and weak areas in our lives. The weak points are the areas He actually likes to hone in on so that we can be made strong disciples. This is not Him picking on you. It's Him promoting you. Letting Jesus lead requires that we allow Him to transform these places that would otherwise limit us.

The hardcore commission to follow Christ is for all and is to be carried out no matter the cost. In the gospels, Jesus required His disciples to give up their current position in order to take on a new one. In fact, He said to the fishers of fish, "'Follow Me, and I will make you fishers of men.' They immediately left their nets and followed" (Matthew 4:19-20 NKJV). It was a massive change.

Interestingly, here the phrase *follow me* is the Greek word *mimetes*, which literally means *to imitate*. *Followers* are meant to imitate or copy their master. But, it is more than just dressing like someone else, eating the kind of food they eat, or walking and talking like them. This word is referring to taking on the very being or spirit of that individual.

When Jesus asked us to be His disciples, He was inviting us to come to a place where His will becomes our will. We are not expected to have long hair or wear a robe and sandals like Jesus did, but our lives should reflect Him so that whenever people look at us, they see Him. Spending time with Jesus is essential to the call of a disciple. Jesus ordained the twelve disciples to be with Him. His invitation essentially said, *Come follow me. Come with me. Walk with me. Delight in me. Be with me. Be a part of me. Abide with me.* These men, mostly fishermen, literally gave up their personal occupation to abide with Him.

Following Him means more than merely attending a Sunday morning service. We must be so engrafted in Him that we seek Him daily and interact with Him all day. He will be the first one we say "hello" to in the morning and the last one we speak to at night. And let us not forget about the middle of the day when temptations come and life's pressures rise up, or anxieties begin to overwhelm us. He must be the light that we follow.

Then once we have decided that we will be followers and disciples of Christ, we find ourselves facing the necessity of taking a stand. We are placed in a position that requires determination. Our proclaimed faith is put to the test, and we are drawn out of the flow of passive following. This is where we learn that letting Him lead will often mean facing opposition. In the forthcoming chapters, you will find tools, insights, and roadmaps to effectively carry these things out and discovering what discipleship *truly* is.

CHAPTER TWO

UNCOMMON PRAYER

THERE I SAT in the garage. Picking up a piece of chalk, I drew a circle around myself. I was desperate. Then lifting my voice to the Lord, I said, "God, I want to hear from you. I'm not going to leave this circle until you touch me." The boundary was set and the desire was made clear. After hours of travailing and calling out to God, He began to speak to me.

Here's the truth: if you want to see uncommon results, get into uncommon prayer. Most of us realize that a fervent and consistent prayer life is integral to discipleship, but how many of us are actually hitting our knees and contacting Heaven?

Not only are radical requests met with radical answers, but consistent prayer actually builds character in us. There are intangible results on the inside that prepare us for what God has for us. So many have reduced prayer to "ask and receive," yet in reality, prayer is a process that gives us new internals, new perspectives, and new hearts. Not merely new stuff.

There's no better example of this than the apostle Paul. For years before he went into ministry, Paul spent time with God in the Arabian desert (see Galatians 1:17-18). He prayed, he gained insight, he saw internal transformation. Unlike other church leaders in that day, he did not receive the bulk of the gospel from other apostles. He received it directly from God.

This intimate time of prayer and fellowship positioned Paul to be used in the mighty ways he was used. Without the hardcore, face-to-face discipleship in the desert, he likely would be ill-equipped for the ventures he went about in his life. Prayer is not a nice bonus to a good ministry. It is the foundation of good ministry.

Think Radically

No doubt, Paul became one of the most hardcore men of God in the New Testament. He had tremendous revelation as well as tremendous difficulty. He was abandoned, beaten, betrayed, starved at times, shipwrecked, and stoned. In today's time we might call his ministry a disaster. On one occasion, after being captured, he was put on trial for his life. His head was literally at stake. The 26th chapter of Acts details the aftermath.

Paul was in a courtroom where everyone there was against him, and he decided to speak for himself. He was not thinking about being set free. Instead, his mind was set on making a passionate defense of the gospel. He decided to go *hardcore* right then and there. The defense was memorable to say the least:

> My manner of life from my youth, which was spent from the beginning among my own nation at Jerusalem, all the Jews know. They knew me from the first, if they were willing to testify, that according to the strictest sect of our religion I lived a Pharisee. And now I stand and am judged for the hope of the promise made by God to our fathers. To this promise our twelve tribes, earnestly serving God night and day, hope to attain. For this hope's sake, King Agrippa, I am accused by the Jews. Why should it be thought incredible by you that God raises the dead? (Acts 26:4-8 NKJV)

In the middle of a courtroom, with his life on the line, Paul took the opportunity to think radically. He was not bellyaching about his capture, weeping or worrying about what was going to happen next. He was not urgently sending out messages to colleagues to bail him out. Instead, he knew there were people inside the courtroom with him, which meant he had an audience. When he had an audience, it meant he had an opportunity. Paul seized the moment to testify of the goodness of God.

This sort of opportunism does not happen by accident. It happens when prayerful people are supercharged by the

Spirit and ready to pounce on opportunity in a moment's notice.

Although he was before one of the chief priests who accused him of being crazy, Paul chose to look at King Agrippa and began to preach to him directly. In other words, Paul was more concerned about the king's soul than his own life.

Paul shared his story of how he persecuted the church until that divine encounter with Jesus on the Damascus road. He spoke with fire of his conversion and his mandate to preach to the Jews, then to the Gentiles, of repentance, and that Jesus was the Christ. His message was passionate and moved the King:

> Now as he thus made his defense, Festus said with a loud voice, "Paul, you are beside yourself! Much learning is driving you mad!" But he said, "I am not mad, most noble Festus, but speak the words of truth and reason. For the king, before whom I also speak freely, knows these things; for I am convinced that none of these things escapes his attention, since this thing was not done in a corner. King Agrippa, do you believe the prophets? I know that you do believe." Then Agrippa said to Paul, "You almost persuade me to become a Christian." And Paul said, "I would to God that not only you, but also all who hear me today, might become both almost and altogether such as I am, except for these chains." (Acts 26:24-29 NKJV)

Governor Festus was shocked to hear Paul's defense, and said Paul was out of his mind. The people in the courtroom calling Paul crazy, nuts, and even brainwashed did not faze him. His goal was to convince King Agrippa of the truth. Paul believed and preached that only the Word of God and the Holy Ghost can cleanse and free people from a messed-up mind full of evil thoughts. These Jews were trying to quench the zeal of this hardcore man of God. They said that he was beside himself. They made similar statements about Jesus. And if you make the right moves, they will say the same of you also.

People are okay with believers in Christ who are excited about business, education, money, school, sports, and other such things. It is a different story when we get radical for God. Lovers of God get branded as right-winged, conservatives, radicals, or fundamentalists. This hardcore passion, however, is what makes our principles of Christianity and witnessing come alive not only for us but for those that hear the gospel. The fervency, fire, and passion ignite the written Word. It is more than just speaking words and handing out church invitations. It pulsates within us, evidence that we are being given Divine help and opportunity to tell someone about Jesus. Do not pass it up.

The very reason that Paul was able to preach with passion and leap on a ripe opportunity is the relationship with Jesus that he had built ahead of time. If you are waiting for the right moment to pray, the right moment will never come. We are called to connect with God as prayerful, faithful sons and daughters, and in that place we will be equipped for all things.

Submarines regularly plunge into the depths of the ocean. How are they able to handle the sheer pressure of the water in those deep places? It's not because the submarine is made of ultra-strong material. That's only part of the equation. The truth is, before a submarine goes under, it is pressurized from the inside. When the sub is pressurized with equal pressure internally as it will feel externally, it's ready to go deep.

This allegory was true in Paul's life and it's true in ours as well. If we want to handle the hardships, abandonment, and pains of life and ministry that come from the outside, we'll need to be pressured from the inside by fervent prayer.

A Prayer Life

Several years ago, I withdrew to be alone in the mountains. It was a seven-day fast, designed for me to do nothing but pray and seek God. On the sixth day, I ran out of things to pray for. Having prayed and said everything I could think of to God, with no one else to talk to, and one more day to fast, I was uncertain about what to do.

Suddenly, in that place, God began to remind me of my old punk rock friends whom I had not really thought of or prayed for in 17 years. That sixth day, I began to pray and weep for those guys and girls. Everyone whose names I could remember, or just the faces I recalled, I included in my prayers.

Afterwards, I reminded the Lord that I had not seen these people since I got saved and if possible, I asked Him to bring them to me so that I could witness to them.

Two months later, I received an email from a girl I knew from a long time ago, which said, "Hello buddy." I showed it to my wife, and then recognizing that this was an answer to my prayers, I replied. She emailed back giving me an update on my old friends. Some had died, and others were in jail. My old roommate had just died of a heroin overdose, and on and on the sad news went. I responded by inviting her to come and hear me preach at a church near her in California. From then until now, I have seen at least 50 of them get saved, and some are now attending church.

During a conference at that church I was preaching the offering message, and when I got off the stage, a guy in the corner motioned for me to come to him. "Come here." I walked over.

He started, "You don't remember me," but I indeed recognized him instantly.

"James! What's going on, man?"

"I can't believe this is happening," he said. "I've never been here before. I was talking about you today to my mom. I thought you were dead. Some guy invited me to this conference and I'm sitting up there," he said gesturing toward the balcony, "and all of a sudden they go, 'Here comes Pastor Kelly Lohrke!'"

I won't tell you the language James used, but he said, "I almost *blanked* my pants, and here you are!" He came back later with his mother to hear me preach, and she got saved.

His whole family is now born again and attending Omar's church. When I saw her respond to the altar call, I said, "It's so good to see you, and I'm sorry if there's anything I ever did to you."

She responded with, "Well, you did break out the windows in my house one night at three in the morning."

God made all things new, single-pane windows included.

Travailing on the sixth day of the fast was a critical point for me. Prayer works. It brings revival. God needs some hardcore men and women who will pray. Pastors, get up and pray for your city! Pray that God will give you some souls, and that God will pour out revival.

Stephen, in the book of Acts, was radically hardcore. He had the same effect with power and passion for God upon his life, enabling him to preach and pray during his last moments on earth. People had stones in their hands, ready to kill him, and he kept on preaching (see Acts 7:54-57). Such boldness to witness while threatened with death comes from a hardcore lifestyle of prayer. "Confess your trespasses to one another, and pray for one another, that you may be healed. The effective, fervent prayer of a righteous man avails much" (James 5:16 NKJV).

God needs radical people that will pray, not emergency flare prayers, but bonafide fervent cries from the heart. Prayer is not just a thing Christians do to pass the time. Prayer is not to be some ritual to carry out in a little corner but is to be full of passion. Crying, weeping in God's presence, and praying in the Holy Ghost are essential to a life of prayer. It is not just a religious duty but our very connection with God.

I won't pretend that this is the only book in print that draws attention to the power of prayer. In fact, because there are so many amazing resources on the subject, I'll spare you a deep dive into the inner workings of intercession, supplication, thanksgiving and beyond. I will say, though, that a fiery prayer life is the furnace of hardcore discipleship. It sets the temperature and the atmosphere for everything you do—whether you're jumping on an opportunity in a bind like Paul with Agrippa, or whether you're dropping kids off at practice and trying to arrange dinner plans with your spouse. In the big and in the small, in the ordinary and in the extreme, a prayer life sets you up for God's best and nothing less.

CHAPTER THREE

RADICAL WORSHIP

A.W. TOZER ONCE said, "I can safely say, on the authority of all that is revealed in the Word of God, that any man or woman on this earth who is bored and turned off by worship is not ready for heaven."

No truer words have ever been spoken. But does our worship today mirror heaven's?

True worship is not some formalized fanfare. It isn't a routine or a religious rite. It is the hardcore surrender and acknowledgement of everything God is. We must become nothing less than hardcore worshippers. When we come together as believers to exalt the Lord, it is one of the most powerful forces on earth. I am referring to hardcore worship, not half-hearted song-singing. Today, we have become so sophisticated in our praise. We dress up nice, perfect and proper, and do not want to ever look like King David when he worshipped. As the king danced, twirled, and worshiped before God, his clothes were falling off to where he was nearly naked as he danced before the Lord (2 Samuel 6). He did not shy away from weeping and crying during his expressions of worship.

David danced before the Lord with all his might. Yet sometimes we stand still before the Lord with all our dignity. We are so picky and particular about how we like the worship service. Folks often complain about the song or the style. It's too fast or too slow. It's too loud or too quiet. The temperature of the room is too hot or too cold.

How about we shut up and worship God? Let's not mince words or pull punches. The Bible says that God inhabits the praises of His people. There's inhabitation that occurs when we draw close. The problem is that some people spend more time analyzing a song service rather than singing, clapping, lifting up their hands and plugging in.

Throughout Scripture we read that when God's people worshiped the Lord, they danced, and when they stood up to praise God, it erupted like fire shut up in their bones. There was a little bit of zest involved when they worshiped and praised God. Sadly, today we are often afraid to get carried away in our Christianity.

Never mind the fact that some are so excited about football that men paint their bodies, put mustard on their chest, scream, spill their drinks, and look like fools at a game. Yet they come to church and any signs of exuberance and fervor is seen as getting a little too emotional. Showing emotion and uninhibited praise is an expression of a strong love acted out. It possesses a robust joy, and anyone who has risen to the top of their field has been fueled by a hardcore, passionate attitude. Worship is no different.

Football is such a major sport in the US and like many people, I have a favorite team. I am a Raiders fan through and through. Great lessons can be drawn from great coaches and athletes. For example, Bart Starr was a phenomenal quarterback, coached for years by the famous Vince Lombardi at Green Bay.

During an interview he said about his former coach, "I wasn't mentally tough enough before I met Coach Lombardi. I had not reached a point where I refused to accept second best. I was too nice, and he said these words to me, 'I believe that nice guys do not finish first.'"

Starr then recognized that to become a great quarterback, he needed a certain mental toughness. "Coach Lombardi put this inside of me," he added. Starr was implying that in a highly competitive and high-contact sport, someone with a hardcore mental toughness must glow all the time, and their actions should show that intense, burning desire to play to win. They do not tiptoe through the game, avoiding conflict or pain, but they give it their all. This should be our mentality as Christians. We cannot settle for being halfway in. We have got to be all the way in. He was referring to a passionate heart for doing what he does. God is looking today for men and women who will have this kind of hardcore passion.

Miracles can happen when we worship God. Worship Him with reckless abandon, and see His power flow. He can heal our bodies while we are singing and change our attitude before the altar call ever happens. With the passion that only cares that Jesus is watching we can be set free in a worship service or even be filled with the Holy Ghost. The potential is limitless. It's not merely a warm up to the service. It's the main event.

We have to get beyond just going through the motions and rituals. We must remember we are singing to the King of kings and entering into His holy presence. I understand time constraints for church services and the traditional 30 second clap after the last song for some churches, but it makes me wonder. Are we clapping because the song service is over or because we are celebrating the one true living God?

Agression's Edge

Nobody likes to lose. No one can honestly say, "When I compete, I really love losing." We all like to win. My favorite sport is basketball, and for me it is a wonderful time of year when the NBA playoffs start. There is something in basketball that has become more aggressive over the years.

Lately it's not just been about putting the ball in the hoop or about how talented competitors are. More and more it has been about how aggressive the team is to win. That basically sums up the way all sports and other pursuits are now: the more aggressive people are, the more likely they are to be victorious.

People will do a lot to win. When someone enters a contest, they want to win at any cost, ideally without cheating. Politicians will do whatever it takes to get votes during an election. Athletes sacrifice their bodies, families, and time to prepare themselves for victory. They workout and push themselves beyond what the majority of us can imagine. Most winners have this one thing in common—aggression. Whatever they do in life they are not passive about it. When it comes to their goals, they don't leave them sitting on the shelf—they go after them.

I still enjoy boxing, and I especially appreciated Mixed Martial Arts. It's a brutal sport. Obviously, when a fighter goes inside a cage for a match, he or she is not going to be casual about it. The more aggressive and intense fighter usually comes out the victor. Sometimes aggression even goes beyond skill. Though the opponent may be better, the fighter with more heart wins.

What exactly does *aggression* mean?

When I think of being *aggressive,* this is what comes to mind: to assault, to attack, to be combative; ready and willing to take issue or engage in direct action, bold and active without hesitation.

The Bible speaks the same way about God's people. We are the people of God's kingdom, called to be more than conquerors. When we study the Scriptures, from the Old Testament to the New Testament, the men and women of God were audacious! The prophet Elijah was one example, the disciples and believers in the New Testament are some others. Their worship and devotion to the Lord was without pause and without remorse.

God's message was important to them, too important to keep to themselves. Boldly, the early church took it to the streets, thus putting their lives on the line. They were beaten. Sometimes they were whipped and thrown in jail, only to be whipped some more. Then when they got out, they did it again!

Talk about having heart! I like what Paul says to the Philippians, "I press toward the goal for the prize of the upward call of God in Christ Jesus" (Philippians 3:14 NKJV).

Up to this point, as we discussed prior, Paul had been through beatings, scourges, imprisonment, betrayal of friends, and so forth. It is obvious that he placed more value in preaching the gospel than in his own life. In his own words, he counted his life as dung.

The problem with human nature is that we can lose that winning attitude. We can lose it in our worship, in our prayer life, and in our mindset. We start something, and then we get bored with it. This is the reason why God says we need endurance. Even Jesus had to stay focused on the joy that was set before Him when He took on the cross.

God's people want to win, but often we want to approach it like the lottery. We want the win as long as it's easy. The problem is, easy wins are rarely a thing. In a real game or contest it's going to take effort in order to pull out the W. It's going to require some pressing towards the mark. To eliminate confusion, this does not mean I am saying that we are saved by works as some people may contend. We are saved by the grace of God (see Ephesians 2:8). However, the book of James clearly states that faith without works is dead, and our works are the evidence that we have faith (see James 2:26).

Our actions usually are a strong indication of what we actually believe. Let me illustrate it this way. I know several phenomenal piano players. If I ask any one of them to teach me how to play and they tell me to show up early before church for lessons, but I refuse, then my desire to play piano is just all talk. If I really wanted to play the piano, I would show up for the lessons and practice in my off time. When we say we want to do something for God, then we gotta show up! It is not going to just happen. It's going to take a little aggression in our walk with God. This aggression gives us an edge. It fuels our worship. It compels us to approach God and to actually mean business with Him in the process.

Answering by Fire

The showdown on Mount Carmel during the time of Elijah is a type of the day that is yet to come. All of Israel went to Mount Carmel for the hour of God's triumph. The prophets of Baal were stirring up trouble and challenging what Israel knew to be true of God. Elijah was raised up to challenge the challenger. Rather than summarizing the major points, I encourage you to read the text for yourself:

> "Now Elijah said to the prophets of Baal, 'Choose one bull for yourselves and prepare it first, for you are many; and call on the name of your God but put no fire under it.' So they took the bull which was given them, and they prepared it, and called on the name of Baal from morning even till noon,

saying, 'O Baal, hear us!' But there was no voice; no one answered. Then they leaped about the altar which they had made.

And so it was, at noon, that Elijah mocked them and said, 'Cry aloud, for he is a God; either he is meditating, or he is busy, or he is on a journey, or perhaps he is sleeping and must be awakened.' So they cried aloud, and cut themselves, as was their custom, with knives and lances, until the blood gushed out on them. And when midday was past, they prophesied until the time of the offering of the evening sacrifice. But there was no voice; no one answered, no one paid attention.

Then Elijah said to all the people, 'Come near to me.' So all the people came near to him. And he repaired the altar of the LORD that was broken down. And Elijah took twelve stones, according to the number of the tribes of the sons of Jacob, to whom the word of the LORD had come, saying, 'Israel shall be your name.' Then with the stones he built an altar in the name of the LORD; and he made a trench around the altar large enough to hold two seahs of seed.

And he put the wood in order, cut the bull in pieces, and laid it on the wood, and said, 'Fill four waterpots with water, and pour it on the burnt sacrifice and on the wood.' Then he said, 'Do it a second time,' and they did it a second time; and he said, 'Do it a third time,' and they did it a third time. So the water ran all around the altar; and he also filled the trench with water.

And it came to pass, at the time of the offering of the evening sacrifice, that Elijah the prophet came near and said, 'LORD God of Abraham, Isaac, and Israel, let it be known this day that You are God in Israel and I am Your servant, and that I have done all these things at Your word. Hear me, O LORD, hear me, that this people may know that You are the LORD God, and that You have turned their hearts back to You again.'

Then the fire of the LORD fell and consumed the burnt sacrifice, and the wood and the stones and the dust, and it licked up the water that was in the trench. Now when all the people saw it, they fell on their faces; and they said, 'The LORD, He is God! The LORD, He is God!' And Elijah said to them, 'Seize the prophets of Baal! Do not let one of them escape!' So they seized them; and Elijah brought them down to the Brook Kishon and executed them there." (1 Kings 18:25–40 NKJV)

A time will come, according to the Bible, when all the armies of the world will be against the Lord's army. The Bible describes how the Lord will win this great battle. The story of Elijah on Mount Carmel is a herald of a mighty battle that is yet to come. Here was Elijah, the man of God, standing against the king, a nation, and false prophets, yet he showed no fear.

He was turning the heart of the people toward a worshipful experience of the one true God of Israel. Likewise, our extreme devotion to the Lord will turn hearts to worship this authentic King.

Sadly, many people do not believe in the return of Christ. Do we really believe that Jesus is coming back and there is going to be a one world government, an Antichrist, the mark of the beast, and everything the Bible has prophesied? Our beliefs should make us run out of our house to tell our neighbors about Christ and encourage them to get a hold of God. If our understanding of end times does not compel us in this way, something is seriously wrong.

In our story here, Elijah seemingly came out of nowhere, and he was ticked off about what was happening. There is no mention in Scripture of God instructing Elijah to do what he did. In fact, there were many instances in the Bible where God directed people's actions. Yet here, Elijah's actions were inspired by faith. He decided to do something about the direction the nation was headed in.

He instructed the false prophets to make an altar to their god and he let them make their preparations first. They did not even need to flip a coin. Elijah had them take all the time they needed to cry out to their god. But nothing happened. Elijah began to mock them, saying that maybe they ought to be a little louder since perhaps their god was on vacation or asleep.

This was a test of Elijah's faith. After having the false prophets cry out all day with no answer from their god, Elijah decided that it was his turn. Elijah was so confident in the God of Israel that not only did he build his altar, apply the wood, and prepare a bull for the sacrifice, he drenched the entire thing with water until even the trench was full. He was creating an impossible situation for God to display His power. It was faith that couldn't be faked. He wanted to make it even harder so that no one could deny the miracle. The true God was going to answer by fire. The question was, would God answer Elijah?

That is a pertinent question for us today. If we do the will of God, will He answer? We know He is not going to answer disobedience. Still, we wonder if He will fulfill His promises if we obey His Word. If we witness, will He save souls? If we give, will it be given back to us? If we truly surrender and worship without abandon, will God manifest? Perhaps the real question is, if we go all out, will God show up?

At the showdown on Mount Carmel, Elijah stood *alone*. He was not aware of the 7,000 that had gone underground. They were believers in hiding. Later, he bemoaned to God that he was all alone until God revealed to him that there was a remnant that had not bowed to Baal. Today, there are a lot of Christians like this at the proving ground. God wants to use them, but they are hiding. Like the way Peter hid when the Lord was being beaten, these believers are hiding in churches. They do not want to get too carried away. The forces of unrighteousness in this world are in the majority just as it was at Mount Carmel, but the greatest power did not rest in the majority. I've read the end of this story. The Bible tells me who wins at the end, and it is God and His people. This is the side we want to be on.

For Elijah, the proof of the true God would be the one who answered by fire. Why did Elijah say that? Baal was worshiped as the god of fire, the lord of the sun, so surely if any god would answer by fire, it would be Baal. Elijah could have made the proof of the test anything else, but he wanted to prove Baal was a false god. He said that if their god had fire, there needed to be proof. Baal's prophets could not refuse the challenge without admitting they were imposters.

Now, note that it is not beyond the power of Satan to send fire to deceive people. Satan has done that before and will do so again. He sent fire to devour Job's sheep and his servants (see Job 1:16). In Revelation 13:13, the beast will do great wonders and make fire come down from heaven. Satan had the power to bring fire down, but nothing happened that day on Mount Carmel. God had greater power, and He literally bound up the power of Satan's priests. That day the prophets of Baal prayed for a minimum of six hours. Six hours minimum! Elijah prayed for twenty seconds. God can get more done via the brief prayers of His people than Satan can when his own priests travail for hours.

He used 63 words in his prayer. That's all. He poured 12 barrels of water over the sacrifice. Elijah wanted there to be no question that God had done the impossible and proved Himself to be the true God. Then the fire fell and consumed the sacrifice and the altar! Baal was proven to be false. Then Elijah had Baal's priests killed. He purged the country from false doctrine. This was a powerful scene of God showing Himself strong for a man who stood for Him. Likewise, God wants to do great things in your life. I have seen young people come, get saved radically, go through trials, and now have been saved for years without losing their fire. Other times, I have seen people get saved and they start off like a bottle rocket, but they get around the wrong people and burn out. God wants to do powerful things in your church and family. Whether it is getting out there to reach the lost or making sure things function right in the church, God needs passionate people with the boldness of Elijah.

A New Hope

After this fiery standoff on Mount Carmel, restoration came to the nation. You know what happened next? Rain began to fall once again. Rain meant that there was new life—a refreshing new hope for God's people and the nation. The ground that was dry and parched could once again be fruitful. A fruitful life is not going to happen on its own. Without an aggressive faith we will find ourselves in a personal, spiritual drought.

It is amazing how aggressive we can get for things that we want to do. Can we let God translate that kind of passion and zeal for the things of His kingdom? God wants to find people who will be aggressive against their sins and the powers of darkness.

One way we can gauge our faith in God is in the way we

worship. I'm not merely referring to screaming and running around the building during song service. But is our singing passionate? Are our minds on God? Are the words that we are singing really to Him? What about our time in the Bible and in prayer? Is it mechanical, or is there a genuine seeking to know God? Are we bowing with our hearts or just our minds?

Just how did Israel get to the point where they were worshiping a false idol and faltering in their devotion to their God? The road to that end is similar to what is happening today. Somewhere it starts off with somebody saying, *"I'm going to just chill. I'm not going to get all crazy."*

What happens then is this attitude catches on and others start saying, "Well if you're not going to do it, I'm not going to do it," or, *"If that family's not going to do it, why should I have to sacrifice?"*

Instead of listening to what God is telling us to do, we start watching others and are influenced by their indifference. Elijah refused to accept this attitude. Instead of just blending in, he went against the grain. He was trying to find people that would be aggressive to stand against the tide of evil in their nation and the compromise that was prevalent among God's people.

The same need to advance God's kingdom exists today. For people's hearts to turn to God, we need to be the kind of people that will be aggressive in evangelizing this world. We are not going to be perfect, but we need to be radical in fighting against sin. We need to be passionate in our pursuit of God. Paul said that he fought against his old nature.

It warred against him (see Romans 7:13-25). *War* means that there is a fight. The spirit man warred against the flesh, and Paul did not just give in, he fought. Neither did he condemn himself when he fell. He thanked God that when he sinned, he had an advocate with the Father, so he got up, repented, and fought again.

In the Spirit of Elijah

Ask yourself, *Do I carry a spirit like Elijah?*

As born-again believers we are called to challenge society when it turns away from God. I am not talking about toting signs in protest. Rather, we are called to challenge the forces of darkness. We are called to snatch souls from the devil, to reach the lost, and to make a difference in the lives of people. Without radical worship at the core, we will have no significant change of allegiance to bring people into.

What is God going to do in these last days? He wants to bring revival and mighty outpourings of His Spirit in a short time. He wants to do a quick work. I do believe that God is in control of this wicked world no matter how dark it seems. We are here to be brighter than the darkness around us. God wants to flex His muscles. He wants to see people get saved. He wants to see signs, wonders and miracles, healings and outpourings and revival all over the planet. Yet as He does, He does so with worship at the center. In fact, in the Old Testament, the Levites marched in the middle as Israel moved from place to place. The Levites were responsible for carrying the presence of the Lord and ministered in song and music. This can only mean one thing: the presence of Jesus must be the epicenter of any movement. Without worship at the core, we have no momentum, we have no movement.

If we will have the spirit of Elijah we can defeat the darkness and spread our faith in the streets, on the buses, at our jobs, and even in our churches.

Today, most preachers have given up on challenging people to pursue the plan God has for their lives. We have turned our pulpits into hometown buffets. Instead of challenging the congregation to wash the dishes or wait on tables—in other words, to serve—we are creating an attitude that the commandments of God are a buffet we can pick and choose from.

Prosperity? Oh I'll take lots of that. And give me a side of blessing, and a heap of healing while you're at it. Service? Sacrifice? Giving? Oh no, I'll just leave that for someone else. After all, my plate is full, and I want seconds of that prosperity.

While few would admit to this thinking out loud, it's prevalent in the American church. God wants to overthrow the power of darkness in every single life. And not just the "big issues" that we would normally think of, like adultery or bitterness. He wants to overthrow everything within us that desires not to possess a spirit like Elijah's.

Do we really believe God has a plan for everyone's life? If so, then why are so many of us not doing what He has called us to do? Let us move ahead with reckless abandonment in our worship and devotion. May the passion we project in a worship service be the passion we possess when we exit our church buildings. Why? Because God is not depending on those in hiding. The tolerance for covert Christianity is gone. He is using those with fierce faith and bold deeds.

CHAPTER FOUR

INSATIABLE HUNGER

I REMEMBER SITTING in an old, dirty movie theater with about 900 other people and feeling like I was on an amusement park ride. I had the same adrenaline I had felt while riding Space Mountain at DisneyLand, yet this was no roller coaster. But at the same time, it was a genuine, tangible thrill.

Where was I?

Church.

I was saved in that church. There was a hunger for God and high expectation for Him to move. The excitement was palpable for every service.

We were so eager to get there, we would wait in line to get in the building—and yes, there was a line to get into church! We were "Bible pushers," meaning we wanted a seat up front so bad we pushed over Bibles that were used to save seats. In those days, people came ready to participate with enthusiasm. During worship, no matter the song, we would lift up our voices with all that was within us. Songs that declared victory in Jesus would cause us to cry because we believed, experienced and had seen the power of God demonstrated in our lives.

Our pastor would then stand up to preach, where we sat feeling like the coaster was starting to climb as he broke open the Word of God. Would some walk out and forget the service, not perceiving it to be a thrill at all? Sure. Would others, like myself, be marked in an indelible way? You better believe it. What was the difference? *Hunger.*

It's been said that an animal that has tasted human blood may have to be put down eventually. Why? Because once they've had it, they begin to crave it and can become dangerous with that desire.

When God touches our lives, we just can't get that experience out of our heads and hearts, though some may try. When you taste and see the goodness of the Lord (see Psalm 34:8) you will wrestle with your flesh and with God from that point forward. Nothing else will satisfy.

When we are touched on a vertical, God-to-man level, everything changes in our horizontal plane. Friendships and people that are around us are altered. Every area of our life begins to change, including our family situations. We face the choice of fighting and running from it like Jonah, denying it like Peter, or embracing what God is doing like David when he discovered Goliath.

A hunger for a close relationship with God is not just a good idea. It's mandatory. We ought to desire to learn and experience everything we can concerning His kingdom. Nothing else will satisfy the one who has been touched by the blood of Jesus. We can build great empires, seven figure businesses, the biggest homes, and lots of prestige, but these will not compare to the moment when God shows up. People can spend their lives trying to find money, pleasure, and success but nothing compares to the touch of God. The world's richest are dross compared with the glory of God.

When I reflect on my time in the church I was saved at, I see a contrast to what is normative in the greater body of Christ today. Today, we come late and leave early. If Jesus was cleansing temples today, His actions would be seen by many as extreme or hardcore, and rightly so. He was not some mild mannered or indifferent Savior. He was fueled with passion, and He was fueled with radicalness. Even the Bible revealed Him quoting an Old Testament passage that said, "Zeal for Your house has eaten me up." (Psalm 69:9, John 2:17 NKJV). His focus never wavered from His mission because He said that He must be about His Father's business.

Scripture recorded that when He saw the multitudes, He was moved with compassion. Today, would we be moved with complaints? *Why do they need my help? Why don't they just take care of themselves? I'm tired of serving, somebody else can do it.*

The fact is, Jesus had compassion on them because He had a passion for them. He wept over the tomb of Lazarus. He wept because somebody was dead. Are God's people weeping when people die spiritually or in a backslidden state? Understanding the magnitude of His assignment, Jesus' attitude was to do the will of the Father who sent Him while it was day. He never complained about His looming tasks but considered it His meat to do the will of God who sent Him and to finish it (see John 4:34).

Even after being rejected in Jerusalem, He wept over the city saying, "Oh Jerusalem, Jerusalem" and did not let that affect His passionate heart. He put His heart on the line for those who rejected Him. *That* is hardcore. We need a genuine and holy hardcore spiritual passion. The passion of Christ is ours to emulate, not just ours to admire.

There are men and women all over who have had an experience where they were radical for God at one time in their lives. They had a vision burning within them but then time happened. Change happened. A preacher, ministry, or a church hurt them, or their family got them all messed up. Then they backslid. The flesh got the best of them. The devil lied to them, and they ran from God. Now some of them have come back. They are trying, but it is from a distance, without the hardcore passion. Now instead of getting right back to where God wants them, they became softcore. It seemed safer and less risky. This is an apathetic and cold attitude towards God. To become *apathetic* means *having or showing little or no feeling or emotion. Spiritless or becoming indifferent.*

Young people have become more apathetic than ever before. I believe in these last days there is an enemy trying to drain and suck the life out of the younger generation. I thought my generation was bad when we turned away from God and did not care. But this one seems worse. I am not talking about those in the world, by the way. I am talking about church kids. Surprisingly, most American Christians are apathetic towards this important issue called the redemption of mankind.

You might read this and say, *Great. I'm supposed to have a hunger for God, but I don't. What now?* The truth is, if we don't get proper food, the sugars in our body take a hit and it can throw us into a state of losing appetite altogether. How do you gain your appetite back? Eat when you don't feel like it. Pretty soon, you'll experience regular hunger again.

This model from the natural world has merit in the spirit world as well. Likewise, in the kingdom of God, you may not feel hungry. But you need to hunger for hunger itself. You may not want it, but you need to want it. Consume the things of God, regardless of feelings and appetites, and you will find yourself back into a steady desire for Jesus and all that He is.

This sort of hunger is not some random feeling that comes and goes. It is a deep, internal longing. It is a fire that stays lit via the kindling and stoking of the Word of God, prayer, worship, and fellowship. We are called to this hunger, not because God is an egomaniac who needs people to want Him in order for Him to be validated. No, God is secure in His own right. This hunger is for the benefit of humanity. To pine for God is to leave behind the very things that once destroyed you. The added benefits of a hunger for the Lord can't be quantified in a book. Yet I do want to point to one that changes everything.

Trust Issues

It's difficult to trust the Lord without having a passionate hunger for Him first. The other side of the same coin is that it's hard to have a passionate hunger for God without trusting Him first. They go hand in hand. Above anything we can do for God, our trust in Him is what He genuinely desires most. It brings Him the most pleasure. In fact, our very salvation is wrapped up in our commitment to trust Christ and His complete work.

Solomon hit the nail on the head when he instructed us: "Trust in the LORD with all your heart, and lean not on your own understanding; in all your ways acknowledge Him, and He shall direct your paths" (Proverbs 3: 5-6).

I am grateful to have taken steps into the unknown in my life, believing for God to make a way and direct my path. I'll share more on some of those steps I've taken later in the book. Today, my family is doing well, and our church is thriving. Doing the will of God can be scary, but we call it *the adventure of faith* for a reason. You can be blessed for being obedient. Taking short cuts, panicking, and quitting is not the way for you to see the blessing unfold. God cannot fulfill His Word in your life if you quit.

After living for God all these years, I refuse to give in and quit. I love God, but I also have a healthy fear of Him. His Word declares that I am going to be judged for whatever I tell you. For this reason, I am doing what God told me to do, and that includes not withholding the truth from you. I want God's Word to stick to your ribs like a big fat greasy burrito causing you to turn to Him wholeheartedly. I pray to God that this book will not just get people fired up but will spur them to new places of trust and faith.

The first chapter of Joshua makes the reward of trust clear: "This Book of the Law shall not depart from your mouth, but you shall meditate in it day and night, that you may observe to do according to all that is written in it. For then you will make your way prosperous, and then you will have good success" (Joshua 1:8 NKJV). If we are honest with ourselves, we will have no capacity to meditate on the Word, speak it, and observe it, unless we trust the One who spoke it. If we withdraw trust from the Christian life, we end the Christian life.

Prospering in all that we do if we observe and keep and trust God's Word is a promise, not a possible benefit. His Word works, but the manifestation of prosperity may not be in our timing. That is the reason why we do not stop applying His principles. Sometimes we get a bad attitude when we feel like we have been faithful but see no immediate result. God cannot bless bad attitudes. We need to keep believing God's Word and make the necessary adjustments in our lives.

When Paul spoke to the Thessalonians, he commended them for receiving the words they heard from him and welcoming them not as the words of men but of God (see 1 Thessalonians 2:13). When people come to preach the Word of God to you, do not receive it as just some guy's thoughts. Paul acknowledged that the believers at Thessalonica not only received the Word of God from them, but that Word was also producing good in their lives.

The danger is this: when people have been saved a long time, attending church, sitting under the same pastor, they have to be careful that the Word of God and the voice of God through the man of God doesn't sound like Charlie Brown's teacher; *wah, wah, wah*. Familiarity has a way of causing people to forget that the words are from God, not mere man.

Frankly, it takes good old-fashioned discipline to sit and hear a message, jot notes, and stay focused. Getting the Word of God inside and then meditating on it also requires discipline. Regular application of these principles and merely chasing words to tickle the ears also calls for discipline. If you remove discipline from discipleship you have a country club, not a spiritual reformation. The Word of God has got to be lived out with integrity, fear, and reverence.

Later in the Old Testament, Deuteronomy echoed similar words: "Therefore keep the words of this covenant, and do them, that you may prosper in all that you do" (Deuteronomy 29:9 NKJV). This is God's promise for any who want to prosper. We may be out there working hard for the things of this world struggling to make it on the job, desiring God's blessing so that we can take care of our families. But sometimes in the process, we can compromise our integrity and the call of God over our lives. Nothing makes me sicker than to hear a Christian say, "God ain't going to pay my bills!" That belief and statement contradicts God's Word and is a direct rebellion to His Word. The Bible declares and reveals that Jehovah Jireh is the provider. It does not say anywhere in the Scriptures that we have to compromise by not putting God first. He honors His Word.

Back to Joshua. We repeatedly see God linking His action to our obedience. "But take careful heed to do the commandment and the law which Moses the servant of the LORD commanded you, to love the LORD your God, to walk in all His ways, to keep His commandments, to hold fast to Him, and to serve Him with all your heart and with all your soul" (Joshua 22:5 NKJV).

Just maybe God is saying that when we start obeying, He will do what He said He would do. Often we may be trying to get our way with God yet He just wants us to be obedient. We should take inventory of our lives and maintain this mindset. An examination of our lives will reveal anything that would quench our fire or a hardcore passion for souls. We need to lay down whatever distractions that are keeping us from doing God's will. God wants to set us in the right direction. These moments of surrendering to His will appear difficult, but it may mean the difference between fulfilling His purpose or not.

Godly discipline is important and so is our time and talent. When we are in a church doing something for God, it is commendable. Our local church needs us to be present and involved. Gathering with other believers in a church meeting is vital. It is up to us who have children to take them to church, especially if they do not drive. Skipping church teaches children that the church is not important. Parents influence their children by words and actions. Arguments with a spouse and complaining about going to church within the children's hearing are not lost on them. Parental authority is abdicated if the child wants to stay home and the parent allows it, because they can do whatever they want when left at home alone. As a teenager, my son didn't always want to attend church, but it was non-negotiable in our home. His heart posture was his choice but as his parent, I had to do what God told me, and that was to *raise up a child in the ways of the Lord*. Now he is a grown man raising his own family in the ways of the Lord.

We need to honor the Lord's Day again. There are people that died and gave up worldly accolades for the Lord's Day. Eric Liddell, who was depicted in the movie *Chariots of Fire*, was the fastest man in the world at the time. He chose not to run his best race in the Olympic Games of 1924 because it was on Sunday, the Lord's Day. The Lord's Day means it is His, not ours. Many of God's people need their priorities readjusted to sync with God's kingdom principles and not the world's. May this chapter act as a spiritual chiropractor, realigning core values. Without hunger, trust, and discipline, our lives won't look much different than the world.

Staying Radical

Being on fire for God was never meant to be seasonal. It was meant to be perpetual. When God would light the fire on the altar in the Old Testament, the priests were responsible for keeping it burning. Likewise you and I have the role of doing something with the fire God initially lit.

We must remember to continually go back to the well of God and get refueled. If not, we will find ourselves spiritually dead. It's been said that going to church does not make you a Christian. As true as that might be, staying away from church certainly will not help the cause. We are called to gather, and to neglect that is to reject the very definition of the word *Christian,* which means *to be like Christ.*

It is amazing that people say they do not have to go to church to be saved. In actuality, they are more likely to hear the message of salvation at church than out on the streets. Many believe that they do not have to tell people about Jesus so that they might also be saved, nor do they encourage people to read the Bible or pray. And yet, all these actions are indications that someone is a believer. When we are not doing any of these, then disillusion, doubt and unbelief can set in. Soon we will feel like our dreams are dying, and our vision is gone. In this defeated condition we start doing things that we thought we would never do. We abandon the things of God, fall apart, and start giving up.

We see no better example of this all-in mentality than in the life of Epaphroditus. Paul commends him in his letter to the Philippians, saying, "Receive him therefore in the Lord with all gladness and hold such men in esteem; because for the work of Christ he came close to death, not regarding his life, to supply what was lacking in your service toward me" (Philippians 2:29-30 NKJV).

Epaphroditus, who had been doing God's will, was facing an all-in moment. He was sick and almost died. He needed to make the trip to Philippi because Paul was unable to make it. The guy could have quit and had someone else go, but not regarding his own life, he went instead. Though he was banged up and beat up, the team needed him. He took a chance for his brothers. Epaphroditus knew discipline. He knew trust. He knew what it meant to keep the fire going, even when he didn't feel like it.

Let's be real, we need each other. One of the most comforting things is knowing that the person beside you would die for you. How reassuring for them too, if they know that you would do the same for them for God's purpose. The Church has been through some things and we can sulk about the past, or we can move forward and fulfill the call of being a disciple today. This call reminds us to not regard our own lives unto death but to live for a purpose that's above our own pain.

Paul himself, when commending Epaphroditus, probably recognized that same ride-or-die mentality in himself. In fact, he said to the Corinthians, "But let me tell you something wonderful, a mystery I'll probably never fully understand. We're not all going to die—but we are all going to be changed. You hear a blast to end all blasts from a trumpet, and in the time that you look up and blink your eyes—it's over. On signal from that trumpet from heaven, the dead will be up and out of their graves, beyond the reach of death, never to die again" (1 Corinthians 15:51 MSG).

Paul was faced with death, but he was not afraid of it.

He was not bound by the fear of death. Whether he lived or died, it was a win-win for him. His mentality was that if he died, he would be resurrected, but if he lived and did God's will, he would be raptured out of here.

The Bible testifies to that event and the second coming of Jesus. The dead will rise with Christ. We who remain will be caught up, and that's why Paul was confident and bold. He was so hardcore because he was so far from fear. Jesus is coming back, the mark of the beast is coming, and the rapture is going to happen. Keep this truth burning in your heart. Maintain the fire of the Lord within you, and you will adopt this same fearlessness.

These are the last days. Asking people to give their life to the gospel needs to be preached, even though that may not be churchy and politically correct. If we are Christians, we need to truly follow Christ. Knowing these things are coming, we must be immovable, stand our ground, and be steadfast.

One morning while driving to church, a song by Don Potter struck a nerve in me. The tune was called *Who are These People,* and was about Christians that will live during the tribulation, who will be tortured and beheaded for their faith. The lyrics were alive as they swept over my soul. They went, "Who are these people? Where did they come from? Why are you crying? Oh Holy One? They're all dressed in white. And linen was so bright. And I bow my eyes as they slowly walk by. These are the people of the great Tribulation. They are saints that made it right...right through the end. Yes these are the people of the great Tribulation, washed by the blood of the Lamb!"

As I listened, I had an epiphany. There I was, living in America, driving my Cadillac to church, with no threats of persecution whatsoever. The song grabbed my heart. From the Apostle John's book of Revelation, it was a glimpse at the future suffering of Christians being tortured in the most horrible way.

With a lump in my throat, I said to the pastors who were riding with me, "Here we are driving to church in luxury. We have air conditioning. We have lights. We're living an easy life in America and there are people that are going to Heaven bloody, beaten, and sacrificing their whole lives. They are being tortured. They are literally watching their children get killed right in front of their eyes, and we complain?"

When that time comes to the Western world, the believers about to face intense persecution will require more tenacity than that which we see in the church today. Such endurance and strength can only be fostered in the presence of God and by answering the call to be true disciples of Jesus Christ. We, as Christians, have a responsibility today to be passion-filled disciples for God, and to faithfully disciple others for His kingdom.

The Altar Of Repentance

Several years back I read a brochure from a church saying that they will never embarrass people, even vowing to never ask anyone to raise their hand or come up to the front.

I almost felt like an idiot because these are the things that I was doing regularly. Then I remembered that I had seen people's lives changed for God at the altar, and others were set free with a public confession of Christ. There needs to be a place where people can shed their tears and let God restore them when we come together. We have many altars but not enough altar calls.

God knows where each one of us is right now and how far we have gone. Whatever area of struggle it may be that we find ourselves in, He comes to each one of us and His Spirit begins to convict us because He does not want any of us to go too far. When first love is lost and we no longer are hardcore about our relationship with God, that can change. It starts at the altar of repentance. The altar is a place when man meets the hardcore God. It is more than just a piece of furniture. We refuse to do away with altars as many have. In fact, we embrace the chance to change. We embrace the place where God fills us with a hunger for Himself.

It's not about embarrassing people or creating some visual spectacle. It's about recognizing areas that God is placing His finger on, and allowing Him to bring about change. Recognizing and acknowledging sin in our lives is good because those that do are never the same afterwards. Isaiah the prophet was one of those men. He had a vision of the throne of God and the altar: "So I said, 'Woe is me, for I am undone! Because I am a man of unclean lips, and I dwell in the midst of a people with unclean lips. For my eyes have seen the King and the Lord of Hosts'" (Isaiah 6:5 NKJV).

Isaiah recognized that He stood before a holy God, and he was sinful. Repentance and restoration brought him back. Just three verses later he responded readily to the Lord, "Also I heard the voice of the Lord saying: 'Whom shall I send? And who will go for Us?' Then I said, 'Here am I! Send me'" (Isaiah 6:8 NKJV).

His repentance had to do with him realizing that he could not live like a man with unclean lips any longer. He gave in to God and was willing to do and go wherever God wanted him to go. Jesus said if anyone puts their hand to the plow and looks back, they are not even fit for the kingdom of God (see Luke 9:62). The problem is that we consider sin to be drugs, alcohol, pornography, and adultery, but Jesus said that living a half-hearted life is sin also. He described it as hypocrisy. It is a sin to lose your first love. It is a sin to not be on fire for God and to live a lukewarm life. How on fire are we for God? Are we on fire, or are we just smoking? Smoke is the evidence of where there once was a fire but not evidence of the fire itself. In the letter to the church at Laodicea, Jesus had a stark warning for the lukewarm church.

> "I know your works, that you are neither cold nor hot. I wish you were cold or hot. So then, because you are lukewarm, and neither cold nor hot, I will vomit you out of My mouth...As many as I love, I rebuke and chasten. Therefore be zealous and repent." (Revelation 3:15-16,19 NKJV)

He did not merely say, *repent*. He said to *be zealous and repent!* The word *zealous* there in the Greek language derives from the word *fire*. Literally, Jesus was encouraging them to be on fire to repent in this scripture. This letter was to the church. He is speaking the same thing to us today. How long will so many come to church and still be in sin? How long will there be those who willingly sin and ignore God's call to repent? May we finally be hardcore and become the real Christians God has called us to be.

Perhaps you've repented and been baptized with water, or perhaps that is still to come. Wherever you are on your journey, know that being baptized is not just a simple bath. It is a representation of the death, burial, and resurrection of Jesus Christ. Those who are baptized come out of the water differently than when they went in. It is a death to self. It is a new life unto God. It is victory over death and defeat.

Hardcore passion does not dwell in the heart of the defeated. God wants to penetrate hard hearts with His truth. The world needs to see the church become hardcore for God once again. We need to be ignited with a fire and passion that rises up in our souls. We need to be a people that do not settle for just being Sunday morning ritualistic, church-going men and women! We cannot settle for this non-accountable, non-committed, soft, and weak Christianity. Instead, hear these words of Jesus and observe them with unmatched focus: "Anyone who intends to come with me has to let me lead. You're not in the driver's seat—I am. Don't run from suffering; embrace it. Follow me and I'll show you how. Self-help is no help at all. Self-sacrifice is the way, my way, to finding yourself, your true self" (Luke 9:23 MSG).

CHAPTER FIVE

HARDCORE LOVE

AT THE START of the 20th century, William Booth had been pioneering the Salvation Army for decades. As he neared the end of his life, he had been invited to give opening remarks at a Christian convention. Unable to make it in person, he decided to send a telegraph. In those days, telegraph companies charged by the word, and with low funds he needed to keep his message brief.

He searched his mind and heart to find the words that would best describe his mission and the gospel-driven cause of his organization. After some thought, he had boiled down his sermon to just one single word on the telegraph: *Others.*

This short but riveting sermon was then read to the convention where it left an indelible mark. It's not about you. I know, we toss that phrase around like a hot potato, but it has never been more true than it is today. When Jesus spoke of the last days, he said, "the love of many will grow cold" (Matthew 24:12 NKJV). In the face of an icy world, you and I are called to display a fiery love that is out of this world and beyond this world.

It seems so simple, but I feel it is one of the biggest missing elements in Christianity today. Jesus said, "Greater love has no man than this, that he lay down one's life for his friends" (John 15:13 NKJV). Jesus was describing a radical, hardcore love that looks different than earthly love.

Earthly love expects reciprocation. I'll scratch your back if you scratch mine. Biblical love removes the *if* and simply loves with no strings attached. This sort of love rocked the world as Jesus described it, "But to you who are willing to listen, I say, love your enemies! Do good to those who hate you. Bless those who curse you. Pray for those who hurt you. If someone slaps you on one cheek, offer the other cheek also. If someone demands your coat, offer your shirt also. Give to anyone who asks; and when things are taken away from you, don't try to get them back. Do to others as you would like them to do to you. If you love only those who love you, why should you get credit for that? Even sinners love those who love them!" (Luke 6:27-32 NLT).

Now, we can all say *amen* to that, but finding people who are actually treating each other in this manner is not easy, even in the church. Jesus challenged us by saying that if we want to be radical for Him, quit loving our own friends only. Loving our own little cliques is easy, but to love the body of Christ, our family, and those that nobody else loves is challenging. Being able to love our enemies, and those who lie and talk bad about us, is a supernatural work that God does through us. You are not responsible for conjuring up this love from scratch. It's a work of the Holy Spirit. In fact, Paul said, "But concerning brotherly love you have no need that I should write to you, for you yourselves are taught by God to love one another" (1 Thessalonians 4:9 NKJV).

Make no mistake about it, though, hardcore love is not always cozy and soft. This type of love builds in us a zeal for God's heart and God's house. Jesus Himself was the kindest, most loving One to ever grace the earth, and that very love meant an intolerance for certain things. Look at Jesus' attitude when He came to the temple and saw what was happening.

> "When He had made a whip of cords, He drove them all out of the temple, with the sheep and the oxen, and poured out the changers' money and overturned the tables. And He said to those who sold doves, 'Take these things away! Do not make My Father's house a house of merchandise!'" (John 2:15-16 NKJV)

He saw complete disrespect going on. He saw irreverence and the misuse of the very purpose of God's house. Today we sure have come a long way, but there is still disrespect happening. If He came to our churches today, what would He see? He might see people playing video games, passing notes, constantly getting up and being disrespectful, or wearing their hat in church. We are so far away from where we need to be that a "whip of cords" is needed to get His house in order. Where is the reverence? When I preach at many churches, it is amazing how people are not captivated by worship or the Word of God. Many of them have the facial expressions of someone doing time in the county jail.

My prayer for preachers is that God would give His ministers radical boldness to preach the real Bible without fear of losing people. The Bible has a dire warning about losing our hardcore lifestyle, our passion or our first love. Look what Jesus said to the church: "But I have this [one charge to make] against you: that you have left (abandoned) the love that you had at first [you have deserted Me, your first love]" (Revelation 2:4 AMPC).

He was addressing the church, the orthodox church and charging them with forsaking Him, their first love. The definition of *orthodox* means that the people *hold the right opinions, the right beliefs, and the right doctrines*. This was called the *faithful church* in the book of Revelations. They were faithful, but they were apathetic, calm, cool, collected, passionless, unmoved, and had not been reaching out to the lost. Follow-ups on loved ones or a brother or sister in Christ were abandoned, figuring somebody else should do it. The church might have been going through the motions, but their hearts were not in it anymore. Gone was their love for God. They had become more concerned about self.

Unfortunately, many believers today are in that same condition. Though Jesus promised that He will never leave nor forsake us, we have left Him. We have left that first love. This is something God has against us. Good things may be going on, and we may be doing everything right, but we have lost something. How many of us remember when we first met Jesus? Do we recall when we first got saved?

I was touched and changed by God in the 80s. I have been serving God since 1987 and just like everyone else, I have been tested. There is a strategy of our enemy, the devil, to cause us to lose that first love. Christianity is made to appear boring, and full of self-pity. The Christian life is made to be all about us when it is not supposed to be that way at all. It is about everyone else but us. When we are already saved and filled with the Holy Ghost, what more do we want? If God blesses us, we are blessed.

Our call is to return to our first love, Jesus, and in doing so, His loves will become ours. We will begin to care about the things He cares about. We will take on His burdens and carry His heart. For those who love Jesus, a passion for lost souls is not optional.

Souls, Souls, and More Souls

William Booth's ministry was about *others* from the get-go. It was not just a place to thrift clothes and furniture like today. It began in a powerful revival. At one point Booth stood before King Edward II and was asked if there was anything that Booth wanted or needed. Booth replied, "Your majesty, some men's passion is for gold, some men's passion is for fame, but my passion is for souls."

One hundred years before William Booth shook the

UK, groundwork was laid by a revivalist named George Whitefield. On one occasion, a Scotsman named David Shane, an agnostic, was seen walking into the church where George Whitefield was preaching and his friend said, "I did not know you believed this message." To that Mr. Shane replied, "I don't, but that man Whitefield does, and I can't stay away from him."

There is something about being hardcore with a passionate zeal for God that makes you like a magnet to people. It draws them. That is the spirit of a soul winner, someone who is passionate for world evangelism, and who actually believes what the Bible says. They believe and preach the living Word of God in a way that catches the interest and attention of people—even the unbelievers.

Jesus did not mince words when He commissioned His people: "All authority has been given to Me in heaven and on earth. Go therefore and make disciples of all the nations, baptizing them in the name of the Father and of the Son and of the Holy Spirit, teaching them to observe all things that I have commanded you; and lo, I am with you always, even to the end of the age. Amen" (Matthew 28:18-20 NKJV).

The harvest of souls really is the motivating factor of discipleship. This is where the church often fails. Discipleship is the Lord's way to reach the world. It is the Lord's way to build a great church. We populate heaven the same way. Discipleship is the key to ministry, multiplication and fulfilling our God-given destiny. We were not created and saved just to get out of Hell. God's touch can minister to our hearts in such a way that what He pours into our lives, we pour into others as well.

The fire with passion for God is kindled and fueled from a love for souls. I know I sound like a broken record to people who know me. *Souls. Souls. Souls.* But the fact is, I am a Soul man. Let me be straight up for the people that cannot stand that about me. Jesus was a Soul man. He came and died for souls, and the only commission He gave the church was to *go into all the world, preach the good news, and make disciples*—simply to reach souls. God bless you for your giving money in the offering at your church. Keep doing that. But Jesus said for you to go and make disciples. He did not say to just clap when *others* go. He said for *you* to go. The commission is not just for certain people or for the five-fold ministry. This commission is for everyone, including you and me.

The church I pastor, called *The Cure Church*, consists of messed up people who are saved by grace. Being that I too was given grace by God when I got saved, I understand the need for it. This was the view of the famous composer Beethoven when he worked with other musicians. He was never upset nor troubled when a performer struck the wrong note. He only became angry if the performer failed to do what Beethoven called *losing the spirit* of that piece of music. Playing a wrong note or missing it was allowed but missing the spirit of the piece was not.

There is one thing that should unite us and that is we have all played some wrong notes in our lives. Even since we got saved, we have made some bad decisions. We have all made mistakes and have all missed the mark, but what is important is the spirit in which we play. Believers must play the same song in unity, which is to go, compelled by love, into all the world and make disciples. We have become satisfied with just playing the right thing sometimes. Being technically correct at doing ministry has become so much of a concern that we have missed the spirit and the heart of what we are all about.

Our Network is known for being passionate, especially when it comes to reaching the lost. We realize people will visit our church, and we love it when people come as our guests. They hear about our church like anyone else, and they come to check it out. We believe and preach the full gospel. I believe that God delivers, heals, and sets people free. I also believe in the prosperity of God and that He wants to provide. Though at the same time, I believe in a balanced gospel. The weightier mission of our church is to reach the lost. We are here to reach sinners and backsliders for Jesus Christ.

While we love and welcome those who are already saved, our focus is to reach the unreached. Beyond all of our instruments, lights, videos, and nice padded chairs, we want souls. If we peel away all the fluff and programs of modern Christianity, we are here to save people from hell. At the end of the day, all the books, cappuccinos, and the t-shirts we sell pale dramatically in comparison to the true mission. The mission is all about saving people before Jesus comes back. We want to go out in the world and reach the lost at any cost, which is why we love to take evangelism out on the streets.

Once, during a conference, a pastor in our church called me from the hospital to say that his sister had been rushed there and she was unconscious due to multiple heart attacks. He did not think that he was going to make it to the conference. Immediately, I told him to get off the phone and go to her, right then and there, to lead her to the Lord! Her eternal destination was at stake because no one knew what would happen with her health. It was a hardcore act. It was not time to grieve and plan funeral arrangements. It was time to snatch a soul out of the fire.

Later, he texted to tell me that he led his sister to the Lord. He said when he began to speak in tongues, the nurse looked at him like he was crazy. Probably like how Festus must have looked at Paul. Sadly, there are some Christians that will let their family die and go to hell because they are too embarrassed to pray for them in front of a nurse. They are religious people who do not understand because they do not have a passion for God or understand eternity.

Jesus is calling us to radical love and obedience in the area of evangelism and influence. We are to break religious norms for the sake of the kingdom and for the sake of lost souls. In Matthew's gospel, Jesus said, "Your ears are open but you don't hear a thing. Your eyes are awake but you don't see a thing. The people are blockheads! They stick their fingers in their ears so they won't have to listen; they screw their eyes shut so they won't have to look, so they won't have to deal with me face-to-face and let me heal them" (Matthew 13:15 MSG).

May our eyes and ears be open, not to cultural norms and dead religious ceremonies, but to the living King who longs to shake up and wake up our generation. Lives are at stake.

A Word for the Leaders

What happens when we begin to lose our radical edge? We become ashamed of God. Us leaders need to be careful that we are not ashamed of the God we serve! If we are more concerned about ourselves and our church looking good, then we ought to move and let God take over. Can the Holy Spirit have His way? Does our church activity resemble the book of Acts, or does it resemble a professional, sophisticated corporate meeting? People should be filled with the Holy Ghost without us being afraid of what others think.

Today, we spend so much time on jokes, illustrations and all the things we add trying to communicate the message so that people can digest it, that we have watered it down and emptied it of its effect. The pastor should have a greater fire to see souls get to Heaven than anyone in the church. Let us take John Wesley's advice when he was speaking to young pastors getting ready to go into the ministry, in regards to the passion with which they were to preach. He said to *set yourself on fire and people will come watch you burn.* Of course this was not literal. For us today, this does not mean we have to sweat or scream, but when sharing the gospel, we better do and say what God wants with conviction and fervor.

Occasionally a murder will occur fairly close to our home church. There are people in our congregation that even know some of the people involved. I urge my church not to see these people as just another crime statistic. We cannot continue to see people as statistics of just another murder in Chicago or St. Louis. We cannot see people as just another statistic of child abuse, kidnapping, or rape. The truth is that somebody is going to spend eternity in hell if they don't repent at the foot of the cross. Pastors, we are not to ignore our calling and the power of the gospel that we carry. May love propel us into the darkest places of our cities, to bring much needed light.

If we ourselves are not being biblical disciples, we cannot move into a place in Christ where we fully develop or fulfill our purposes. Without being biblical disciples, souls will not become a major priority in our lives. If we believe we are called by God, and that He has placed a destiny over our lives, then we cannot just sit on the sidelines or be content to just be church attendees. Our determination to fulfill our destiny will all flow from an understanding of what it means to be true disciples.

Real Christianity is not about our will but the will of our Heavenly Father. What is God's will for us? We might not know, which is what I usually hear from people. They promise that they will do anything or go anywhere that God asks them. That is easy to say, but what about His simple will right now? We are not talking about God's will for you one day, far away, but His will for you *today*. How about living a clean life? Start by dealing with the bad attitudes and habits, gossiping, lust, mistreating a spouse, being non-committal to the things of God, pornography, gossipping about leadership, and uncontrolled anger? What about not sleeping with a girlfriend or not cheating on a husband? These are things that God wants to deal with in our lives.

What about being a disciple in the things that are considered not so important today? Tithing and giving offerings for instance, which, if we are not doing, the Bible says we are thieves (see Malachi 3:8). There are those that basically do not trust God with what belongs to Him and have come up with their own theology that excuses them from what God wants them to do.

The call to be a disciple is the call to live holy for God, regardless of your station in life. The Bible declares that without holiness no man shall see God (see Hebrews 12:14). The call is clear. Jesus said, "Not everyone who says to Me, 'Lord, Lord,' shall enter the kingdom of heaven, but he who does the will of My Father in heaven" (Matthew 7:21 NKJV).

Jesus was addressing everyone here, especially those who claim to be His disciples. Calling Him *Lord* does not guarantee an entrance into the kingdom of God. Heaven is for the ones who do the will of the Father. Are we doing the will of God? Nowhere in the Bible does it say that we have to say a certain prayer to be saved. Not to disappoint some of us, but the sinner's prayer is not in the Bible. Someone created that for us to grasp the born-again experience. The sinner's prayer is just the beginning of a surrendered life and not the end.

We have Christians today that believe once saved, we can do whatever we want. Jesus said the opposite, which is to *do* the will of the Father. The word *do* is an action word. We have to do something, but not just anything. Our will takes a back seat to the will of the Father if we want to make it to Heaven. Some people might excuse this as just Jesus being legalistic. To be honest, most of us probably could not cut the mustard if Jesus was our pastor.

Several years ago, I got a hold of this book called *Jesus Mean and Wild* by Mark Galli that really fired me up. I do not necessarily agree with everything I read in books, except the Bible or the books I write, but, what was exciting in this book was that it dealt with all those hard things Jesus said that many people, including pastors, gloss over. The book highlighted all those tough verses where Jesus was not as passive and laid back about people following Him as we've made it today.

Attending church will not help if we are not doing the will of God the Father. People can get offended at this, but this was the message of Jesus. The reason is because churches today are preaching that God does not care about how you and I live. For too many years, we have lived under a system that taught people about what God will do *for* them instead of what God will do *through* them. The focus is on a God that wants to give us everything we want and does not ask for much in return. We have turned God into a game show host, a genie, or a scratch-off ticket. But God is not like that, and that is not the message of the gospel. The true gospel is that we deny ourselves. True followers of Christ seek to do the will of the Father. Christ said, "Anyone who isn't with me opposes me, and anyone who isn't working with me is actually working against me" (Luke 11:23 NLT).

These are Jesus' own words. It may sound shocking to us today because we have been fed spiritual junk food. We have been listening to garbage on Christian television, the internet, and radio. Or we have formed our own golden calves of theology, customizing it to fit what we think. There is no middle road. If we are not working with Jesus then we are working against Him.

Even some of His disciples said this call of discipleship was too hard. Wanting only the free stuff and the fun stuff, they rejected the surrendered stuff. Jesus had multitudes following him. They were present when He multiplied the fish and bread. He was healing everybody. Talk about universal healthcare! Free food and free healthcare. Those that came just for the handouts of food and free healthcare were weeded out the day Jesus said, "If you don't eat my flesh and drink my blood you can't be my disciple" (John 6:53 NLT). What was the effect? "At this point many of his disciples turned away and deserted him" (John 6:66 NLT).

Many disciples left him. Not just a few! This is the same mindset we encounter today when people say, "I want to go to church but I don't want to be a fanatic and start preaching about this like other people." Truth is, there is no middle ground. Jesus said, "No one can serve two masters. For you will hate one and love the other; you will be devoted to one and despise the other. You cannot serve both God and money" (Matthew 6:24 NLT).

Isn't it funny that we are really good at serving money? We cannot worship the true God and be a willing slave to the god of money. We will sacrifice our families, time and even our relationship with God for the almighty dollar, especially because it is so scarce today. I believe there is a reason why this is happening to the American economy. The Bible prophesied that there is coming a day when a bag of gold will buy a loaf of bread (see Revelation 6:6). It does not sound like a great economy is coming, but this will also weed out those that are serving God just for what they can get out of Him.

Consider taking a fast from the world so that you can discover the vision of the kingdom of God. The time to go all out for Jesus is now. Be a Soul man or woman. Be a disciple. Take on a heart of fierce love and watch God reorder your priorities. If we want to see a harvest like we have never seen, we must commit ourselves to the harvest field like we never have before. Souls worldwide are depending on it.

CHAPTER SIX

REMAINING TEACHABLE

WHEN I GOT saved as a teenager, our church did not have a youth group so we were discipled right alongside the adults. Young people were hungry to walk in God's will for their lives—in fact, by the time they were 17 or 18 years old it was commonplace for them to be leading Bible studies.

As a young disciple myself, I was given a nickname by the Hispanic brothers in my church. They called me the "White Shadow" because I was always with my leader. He didn't have to call me or hunt me down, and I honestly felt my leader was not supposed to follow me around. I was supposed to follow him as he followed Christ (see 1 Corinthians 11:1). Jesus said follow after the lost sheep, meaning we leave the 99 to find the one that is lost. I wasn't lost. I was a disciple. So my expectation was not to be tracked down by my pastor but to hang close, gleaning what I could.

Similarly, a son follows after his father. When he doesn't know what to do a son gets advice from his father. When he messes up he gets corrected by his father. A son sits and listens when his father wants to speak into his life, and when a son is hungry he'll come home and eat.

Do you want to be a disciple? Then be a learner. Be teachable, and allow someone who is seasoned and godly to lead and mentor you. Then go and mentor someone else. Every move of God, without exception, has been fueled by this radical hardcore lifestyle of witnessing, worshiping, giving, praising, loving, and mentoring. All of these features should be chock full of passion and radicalness.

Wilbert Hodgeskins, a pioneer missionary in Africa, was someone who showed this kind of passion for God. While looking back over 40 years of his life, he said these words: "I've been 49 times with a fever, three times afflicted by lions, several times by rhinoceros, but let me say, I would gladly go through the whole thing again if I could have the joy of bringing Jesus to the tribes of Africa." Where are those radical people today, the kind of people that are willing to put everything on the line? We need to seek this, cultivate it, and protect it at any cost.

When I was in the early stages of being mentored and discipled, I pulled on my leaders—asking questions and opening myself to accountability. The truth is, though, that teachability has had to remain in my life. We never outgrow a need for leadership. Often, some feel that a novice needs discipleship and mentoring, but a veteran has somehow grown past it. No, if you feel you've grown past learning, you aren't a disciple at all. From the moment we get saved to the moment we leave this earth we have a relentless, perpetual need to be flexible, pliable, and able to shift on a dime for the call of God. Teachability is the crown jewel of a true disciple.

Re-Vision

What do we do when we carry a vision, but God has a different one for us? How do we respond to the word *no*? How will we respond when we are passionately headed in a certain direction, and the Holy Spirit shuts the door?

Hardcore disciples must want to be led and developed. People that are willing to pivot are pleasing to the Lord. There needs to be a pursuit to know who Jesus really is and what He wants, regardless of our preferences. There should also be enough wisdom to understand what is at stake. Counting the cost, and still determining we are ready to take a particular stance will carry us a long way.

In the church where I was saved, it was no secret that I wanted to go to Chicago to be a pastor. Carrying a burden for that city, for several years my wife and I would go to the library to read up on Chicago and look over maps of the city. I talked to my pastor about it, prayed earnestly, and sported Chicago gear. One day while having coffee with my pastor, he agreed that at our next big conference, six months away, he would announce us to be sent as pastors to the city of Chicago.

But, a couple of months before the conference, he said

that the church in Sacramento, California needed a new pastor and asked me to pray about it. My wife and I did, but we felt no peace about going there. The very next day, I was laid off from my job as a truck driver. During that time, two more churches in two different states extended an offer for my wife and I to pastor, but upon praying through it, we turned them down.

My heart was still set on Chicago.

Three weeks before the conference where the big Chicago announcement would happen, I was still unemployed. And to make matters worse, my car was stolen. Worse yet, we lost our second baby, causing my wife to bleed every day for the next six and a half years. It was tumultuous. The conference arrived and there was a dark cloud hanging over the fanfare. It was announced that we were being sent to pastor in Chicago, but our excitement was muted. We felt beat up.

Everything changed about three weeks later. On a Wednesday night, my pastor approached us and said that he needed us to go to Kansas City. A small church there with two families from our church needed a pastor. We were to leave that Sunday.

Talk about a flood of emotions! Immediately, I began to wrestle with being obedient. Without any information about the city or the church I was headed to pastor, I was scared. At the time, I had never been to Kansas City, and did not know if they even had cars. I imagined dirt roads and everyone getting around in a horse and buggy.

Taking my family into the unknown and being my mom's only child did not ease my fears.

My wife is from a close-knit Cuban family, so leaving her mom weeping in my front yard and my mom on her knees in the street crying was heart-wrenching for all of us. I gave up my house, a church, family, and friends. The drive was about 1,600 miles and we made the trip in two days.

God was redirecting me through my pastor, someone who was in authority over me and watched out for my soul. I had to trust him. The Bible says, "Obey those who rule over you, and be submissive, for they watch out for your souls, as those who must give account. Let them do so with joy and not with grief, for that would be unprofitable for you" (Hebrews 13:17 NKJV). I submitted and was willing to have a re-vision. Beyond that, most importantly, God was in the move—and I knew it.

Being willing to let God burst the bubble of my plans and give me new ones has been one of my greatest blessings in life. It was costly for a moment, but yielded incredible fruit long term. When we feel alone in making a sacrifice for the call of God, know that these sacrifices have been normative from the start of the church. Look at Paul, for example. We know him as the great man of God who wrote two-thirds of the New Testament. But he was a man with a past. He was a man who, for most of his life, had been known as Saul.

He described himself as a pharisee of pharisees. A very learned and passionate man, he set out to destroy Christianity. In the book of Acts we are told that he held the coats of those who were stoning the first Christian martyr, Stephen. Imagine that: he was so calloused to the Christian message, that he held the bulky coats of those executing Stephen so that their range of motion would not be limited with each throw of the rock. While God-fearing men were mourning Stephen, Saul was going house to house arresting anyone who believed in Jesus.

Now, he sincerely loved God. Yet because of this love, he had determined he was going to go all out to destroy this new religion that was turning people away from the faith of Israel and the teaching of the law. It was misdirected zeal.

Saul, full of rage and the intent to kill, obtained letters from the high priest to take to the synagogues of Damascus, granting him the authority to arrest followers of Christ and bring them to Jerusalem. Then, a re-vision occurs.

> "When he had almost reached Damascus, suddenly a light shone all around him. He fell from his horse, and he heard a voice: 'Saul, Saul, why are you persecuting Me?' And he replied, 'Who are you Lord?'" (Acts 9:3-5 NKJV)

The reply must have been shocking to Saul: "I am Jesus, whom you are persecuting" (Acts 9:5 NKJV). The Lord then told him to go into Damascus and wait for further instructions. There was a catch though. When Paul got up from the ground he was completely blind. At the same time, this was the beginning of Saul gaining his ability to *truly* see. This awesome encounter with Jesus on the way to Damascus was just the start of Saul's re-vision.

He had killed people in the name of God and was carrying a vision and authorization to further the persecution of the church. God was about to turn that around. What was interesting was that Saul was blinded, and radically touched before God told him to go somewhere. God had to blind him and take away his security. The men who were with him led him into Damascus. When God knocks someone off their high horse it's because it's time to be discipled. This will not happen if they will not allow someone to guide them along the right path.

One of the most interesting things that happened to me when I first got saved was that I was, in a sense, "blind" for a while. I lived in a garage and nobody knew where I was. Since I had been on crystal meth, the guy that lived in the front house, now a dear friend of mine, Pastor Menchaca, had to take me by the hand to church the next day. Three days later after being on crystal meth, he had to guide me on an outreach. He had to guide me to his living room, read me the Bible, and teach me about God. For a time, he woke me up in the morning and taught me how to pray.

Saul needed someone. After three days without eating or drinking God told a man named Ananias to go pray for Saul to receive his sight. Ananias hesitated. After all, this was the man who was killing Christians. But God said, "Go, for he is a chosen vessel of Mine to bear My name before Gentiles, kings, and the children of Israel. For I will show him how many things he must suffer for My name's sake" (Acts 9:15-16 NKJV).

Ananias was a devout believer in the early church but was only reaching people like him who were Jews. *Ananias,* in Greek, means *the Lord's gracious gift* and he truly was God's gracious gift to Saul who was on a road to destruction. The word *grace* occurs 125 times in the New Testament. Of those times, 120 were written by Saul, now known as Paul. After he was touched by somebody who showed grace, Paul not only showed grace to others, but also taught it and wrote it.

Ananias in Aramaic means *God is merciful.* God was about to show mercy to Saul and asked Ananias to live up to his own name. Ananias represents the church in this story. Are we, as the church of Jesus Christ, showing mercy and grace? God could have healed Saul on his own, but He chose, and still chooses, to let His people be part of His plan. Ananias was teachable. He allowed God to disrupt his ministry schedule.

The truth is, like with Ananias, God can bring people into our lives that might scare us because of where they live, the color of their skin, or the uniform they wear. It is possible that God is bringing them to us so that we can show them mercy. Maybe they are confused about who they are as people and need salvation and healing. True, we need to be safe and use wisdom, but the church should not be fearful. We are not to be afraid of those that He brings into our lives.

If we show mercy and love to people, God can raise

them up radically fast. He can do a quick work in them. This is no knock on those who are still struggling as Christians, but when God showed the truth of the gospel to me, one prayer set me free from all my addictions. From then on, I never got high, never stuck a needle in my arm, never smoked a cigarette, or drank. I know that may not be everyone's testimony, but it certainly is mine.

Not too long after I was saved, I was preaching on Pacific Boulevard and Huntington Park, on the main drag. Years prior to that, I was on that same street at a punk rock concert doing a stage dive. That stunt is actually in a documentary. Now, here I was, in the same venue, saved and sharing the gospel. There were two cholos listening, who were as high as they could be on either PCP or angel dust. Though they were fried, I could see that they were convicted, so I offered to pray with them. I believed that God was going to sober them up. Within five minutes one of the guys was sober, and his eyes were normal. I began preaching, and he was interpreting for me in Spanish.

Anyone can immediately be set free if they will allow God to give them good vision. The guy who let me live in his garage had no idea that I would be pastoring a church, much less leading a Network of churches years later. He had no idea that the messed up 19-year-old in his garage would be traveling all over the world preaching the gospel. And he certainly had no idea that the church I pastor would minister through a drama that has preached the gospel to over 80,000 people. What he saw then was just a blind and lost young man on the road to destruction.

Back to our friend Ananias. He went from the encounter with God and found the house where Saul was staying. He went inside and laid hands on him, saying, "Saul, my brother, the Lord Jesus, who appeared to you on the road, has sent me to pray for you so that you might see again and be filled to overflowing with the Holy Spirit" (Acts 9:17 TPT).

God is trying to send people to recalibrate our vision. He did it with Saul. Instantly, a crusty substance which was over his eyes disappeared, and he could see perfectly. He got baptized, ate a meal, and within the hour was in the synagogue preaching and proclaiming Jesus Christ as the Son of God. Saul, the bully, the religious zealot was now becoming the preacher of grace. Prior to his conversion, Saul thought he knew God, but what he knew was religion. He had a zeal for Him, he knew tradition, but had a religious spirit that caused him to persecute the church and attempt to hurt the move of God. The Lord had to give him a re-vision from religion to relationship.

Often we can think that we are being zealous for God, but we are just being religious. We can be amazingly wrong and still think we are amazingly right. One must stop from time to time to have a renewing of vision, a re-vision.

God wants to change people's lives. Like Saul, we have to fall off our high horse, bite the dust, and have blinded eyes to have a true revelation of Christ. Otherwise all we have is our ideology, our bickering with one another, and a lack of regard towards the bride of Christ as a whole.

Without teachability, we won't have our eyes opened

like Saul nor will we be in position to open the eyes of others like Ananias. Be flexible in your life and your witness. Be open. Be vulnerable to His voice. Because anything else is a vessel not fit for service.

Follow the Leader

Even though Paul had a radical transformation, and was a young and fired up convert, he stayed in the church for years getting disciplined by the prophets and teachers. Yes, he went to the synagogue preaching and testifying about Jesus, but he also allowed the leaders in the ministry to raise him up. After years of being a disciple, while they were praying and fasting, God finally released Paul to go out and do something for Him. The Bible said that the leaders there fasted and prayed, then laid hands on them and sent them off (see Acts 13:1-3).

The word *sent off* here is a military term meaning *to dispatch*. This was commissioning Barnabas and Paul as apostles. *Apostle* simply means *sent one*. They were sent by the Holy Spirit and the church and released to be missionaries.

Men and women cannot hear the voice of God all by themselves when it comes to major ministry decisions. Scripturally, they need to hear the voice of God from their leaders as well. This happened to Paul when he was first sent out. I know that bothers some of us. Yes, God speaks to us all, but when it comes to leading, God speaks to the leaders.

The books of Exodus, Deuteronomy, and Numbers

show this example. Just because God spoke to Moses did not mean that God did not speak to others that were there too. God spoke to Joshua, Caleb, and Aaron, but it was a confirmation of what God had already spoken to Moses. When we will heed the voice of God through someone else, we will earn the right to hear the voice of God for ourselves.

Paul had a heavy prophetic word over his life. He knew God was going to use him because of the prophetic word, but he would not get ahead of the game. Any great person that did anything for God had somebody in leadership speaking into their life; meaning they probably got rebuked, and became comfortable with phrases like *hold on*, *no*, *not yet*, or *wait*.

Those who think badly about church leadership and do not listen to or respect them will not go far. Listen, the devil will lie and tell people that their leadership is holding them back from the calling of God. Anyone who believes they have a vision to do something for God should remember that no one, not even leadership, can hold a good man or woman down.

I got saved at 19, married at 21, led a small group at my home at 23, got announced to pastor at 25, and rolled into Kansas City to pastor a church right when I turned 26. That was fast, and it does not happen that way for everybody. Even when things were challenging as a young disciple, I had the mindset that maybe God was teaching me something. Things might have turned out much differently if I had responded to my leaders with an attitude or rebelled.

Being correctable and aware of my own ignorance kept me soaking up insight like a sponge. The only people who stop receiving are the ones who feel they are already full. Sometimes correction is not always about sin issues or bad attitudes. Often, leaders need to redirect us for other reasons. For example, as a new convert, the same drive I had toward destruction was turned toward living for Jesus. Some of the crazy things I did in order to witness to people got me rebuked by my pastor. I remember some guys and I staged a fight in a laundromat, and when people gathered around to watch, we started preaching to them.

Another guy and I used to drive around East LA after a small group, looking for backyard parties to crash so that we could preach to the people. We arranged get-away plans just in case the situation got hairy. Preaching at the mall with a friend was a little more challenging. We found that by synchronizing our watches we could preach at the same time at different areas of the mall near exits, avoid security and make a quick get-away if needed. But afterwards our pastor would get these phone calls about what we had done, and we got corrected. Being young and new, I needed to be corrected because I needed loads of wisdom. Solomon wrote, "Enthusiasm without knowledge is no good; haste makes mistakes" (Proverbs 19:2 NLT).

When God Says No

It's easy to grasp God saying *no* to carnal or sinful things like lying, deceptive business practices, or adultery. Those are pills we can swallow. But what about when He says *no* to good things? Paul was no stranger to this. Luke records that, "The Holy Spirit had forbidden Paul and his partners to preach the word in the southwestern provinces of Turkey, so they ministered throughout the region of central and west-central Turkey. When they got as far west as the borders of Mysia, they repeatedly attempted to go north into the province of Bithynia, but again the Spirit of Jesus would not allow them to enter. So instead they went right on through the province of Mysia to the seaport of Troas. While staying there Paul experienced a supernatural, ecstatic vision during the night. A man from Macedonia appeared before him, pleading with him, "'You must come across the sea to Macedonia and help us!' After Paul had this vision, we immediately prepared to cross over to Macedonia, convinced that God himself was calling us to go and preach the wonderful news of the gospel to them" (Acts 16:6-10 TPT).

Paul was eager to preach. He had a heart for the people. Yet this particular region was off limits. When did Paul learn how to handle a *no*? Maybe it was after he regained his vision and preached in the synagogue with the anointing but, shortly after, had made the decision to sit down in the church, grow up and be discipled for *years*. Later, he heard the cry to go over and help the people in Macedonia, which is modern-day Bulgaria in former Yugoslavia. God was essentially using Paul to bring the gospel to Europe.

Paul and the apostles at this point had acquired a kingdom vision, and they responded accordingly. In the King James Version of the Bible, it says that he endeavored to go immediately. That word *endeavor* means to make an *earnest attempt* to try to achieve, to try to do something with the best honest effort. In the Greek, *effort* means *to seek after with everything*. Jesus galvanized this reality forever when He said, "But more than anything else, put God's work first and do what He wants. Then other things will be yours as well" (Matthew 6:33 CEV).

Kingdom priority is an *endeavor of making an honest effort* to try to keep the vision and to do something for God. Kingdom priority has enemies, and the number one enemy I have seen is procrastination. No one can have vision and procrastinate. Procrastination is not only the thief of time, but it is also the grave for opportunities.

So many have heard a message or received some sort of inspiration that got them all fired up. They got all gung-ho and vowed to do whatever it was they were fired up to do. But then something or someone offended them, and feeling let down, they gave up. We all get hurt. That's life. But we must not let go of the vision of God. Not only that, but often people are passionate about the things of God but give up when God says *no* to their own idea of what ministry looks like. I have no doubt that Paul really wanted to preach in the southwestern provinces of Turkey. When God said *no* he could have thrown a pity party and given up. However, that would have cost him the opportunity to experience the fruitfulness of his time in Macedonia.

As a pastor, I cannot control how people live or the timing of God. I have watched people with God's gifting on their lives, and you can see how their heart starts pumping as they get excited for God. But then they start doing this or get into that other thing, and pretty soon the gift is put off. To *procrastinate* is to put off until later what God has been telling you to do now. There is a window of opportunity that can be missed. I have seen people miss opportunities. Do you know that disobedience can send other people to hell? Whatever God says, even if it's just to witness to someone begging for money, just do it. Souls are connected to our obedience.

When God's people have a big vision to do something for God, a pastor or leader is not a genie or some mind reader that can just make that happen. It starts with allowing people to speak into our lives. It's an important thing to spend time with them and learn from them. That is how it happens. In my case, as a young disciple, I chose to get the key to the church and open it up for prayer because I knew the man of God was going to be there.

There is an element of the pursuit of those who God puts over our lives. As a pastor, I stay accessible to disciples. While I know I am possibly opening the door to chaos, I believe that is what I am called to do—disciple others in the faith. I teach my congregation if they want to talk to me, not to preface it with, "I know you're busy." I am busy. But discipling others is a major priority in my life.

In retrospect, my pastor sending me to Kansas City was in fact God's will for my life. The lesson was learning to hear the voice of God in my man of God before I heard from God myself. This was vital for me to know that as a young disciple. Like I wrote prior, I could have responded to my pastor with an attitude, but then I would not be where I am now. My wife and I would not have a church with so many faithful people who in turn share the gospel with others. We would not have had the joy of sending pastors to plant other churches. There would have been no conferences. There would have been no drama ministry that has brought thousands of lives to Jesus. Definitely some of our people, now saved and living a good life, would be in prison or worse. This was all tied to my *yes* to the man of God. It was all tied to being willing to hear *no* to my own vision of ministry in order to adopt God's.

Salvation happens for us at such moments of vulnerability and sometimes brokenness. At the end of a road called "my own way," I found Jesus, and this is true for everyone else also. In that moment where we recognize our own inability, we are truly teachable. We are willing to sacrifice and lay things down. Yet the goal of the gospel is not to create a moment of teachability in us but to create a lifelong internal culture of teachability. Being able to correct course, handle a *no* from God, and embrace change is the bread and butter of a hardcore disciple.

CHAPTER SEVEN

TANGIBLE IMPARTATION

I WAS BORN and raised in Los Angeles. There, every year from late winter to early spring, the rainy season moves in and drenches the landscape. When this happens, green grass pops up. That same grass eventually dries out, browns, and acts as kindling for massive fires in the summer. I've seen a few. In fact, I recall one time while preaching at a church, I walked out of service and looked at the foothills and saw a ring of fire spreading all over. Someone had started with a small flame and set thousands of acres ablaze as a result.

I liken this to our influence in the earth. Just one single person, with the right flame in the right place, can have a massive impact. One person on fire for Jesus can pass their fire to innumerable lives. Now picture this: the Scriptures mention that one can set a thousand to flight and two can set ten thousand to flight (see Joshua 23:10). Most read this and might think that one person putting a thousand to flight joined with another person would mean they could *together* put two thousand to flight. Seems like simple math. But in the kingdom, things are calculated differently. We can do more together than we ever thought imaginable on our own. This is synergy.

From the Old Testament to the New, God has placed emphasis on the value of impartation. By nature, impartation cannot happen with one person on an island. It happens through direct contact and influence. Notice Paul said to the Romans, "For I long to see you, that I may impart to you some spiritual gift, so that you may be established—that is, that I may be encouraged together with you by the mutual faith both of you and me" (Romans 1:11-12 NKJV).

The secret of discipleship is that it is more than reading a book. If we reduce it to that, we are taking the easy way out. Reading on discipleship is something I emphatically agree with and encourage. You're doing it now. Attending church and reading about discipleship, however, will not make you a disciple. Acquiring various discipleship methodologies or dressing like a spiritual person is not going to get you discipled. One of the mysteries of the gospel is that there is an element of discipleship that can only be released via importation.

The Transmission of Grace

Discipleship is not a method. It has been said that it's not about what's *taught*, but what's *caught*. No one is going to catch it sitting at home or by doing their own thing. It's caught by consistently coming to church and surrounding yourself with those who you can learn from. Impartation occurs as a direct result of discipleship in the kingdom of God. We first find this kind of impartation in the story of Moses.

> "And the Lord came down in the cloud and spoke to Moses. Then he gave the seventy elders the same Spirit that was upon Moses. And when the Spirit rested upon them, they prophesied." (Numbers 11:25 NLT)

But this never happened again. God instructed Moses to bring the 70 elders to the tent of meeting and His Spirit, that was upon Moses, was put on them. Notice that it was the Spirit of *God* resting on Moses that was imparted and not *Moses'* spirit. Through this impartation, the elders and Moses became like-minded. Outwardly, the change may not have been seen, but you could watch the effects play out.

Being that it is a sovereign work of God, the process cannot be understood completely. One person gets it and another one does not. A pastor or leader could pour their life into somebody, and they may not do anything with it, but another takes it and runs with it. There is a young man that I know personally who is an example of this phenomenon.

He was just a guy off the street who happened to come to our services years ago. I remember the day that he walked into the church and sat in the back row. He gave his life to Jesus, became discipled in the things of God, and he received an impartation to preach. He now pastors his own church, and you can just see the Spirit of God upon him when he ministers. He was just a regular guy who said he wanted to be a disciple of God and committed himself to the process. He *caught* it.

What was unusual about the story of Moses and the seventy elders was that two of the elders, Eldad and Medad, were not at the meeting, but the Spirit of God still came upon them. Numbers records, "But two men had remained in the camp: the name of one was Eldad, and the name of the other Medad. And the Spirit rested upon them. Now they were among those listed, but who had not gone out to the tabernacle; yet they prophesied in the camp" (Numbers 11:26 NKJV). They were somewhere else in the camp altogether, yet God's supernatural impartation fell upon them too.

Another cornerstone example of impartation is found in the life of Elijah and Elisha. As the prophet Elijah was taken to heaven in a whirlwind of God, Elisha received a double portion of his anointing. We do not completely understand this but simply know that it happened. But how did it happen? Elisha served Elijah; meaning he assisted the prophet, even washed his hands, let him speak into his life, and accepted correction. Elisha surrendered his life and allowed the impartation of Elijah his leader.

Impartation is a *transmitting of grace* from someone's life to another believer in the kingdom of God. As we live for the Lord, we are filled with the Holy Spirit so that we are able to confer or impart who we are to another believer. This includes the best of who we are and the worst of who we are. Those who live for God are an example for others and are imparting good. Those who are rebelling, compromising, or bucking against the will of God, are not only imparting that to their children, but also into other believers. We see other great examples in the Bible of those who imparted good. Joshua and Caleb stuck close to Moses as they moved towards their destiny, and it was obvious the impartation was there. The Bible describes them as having a different spirit compared to the other ten spies who went first into the Promised Land. Both men made it into Canaan because they believed God's promises and followed Moses' leadership faithfully. Another biblical account that showed this principle is the story of Joseph's two sons, Ephraim and Manasseh, that were brought to Jacob for a blessing.

Jacob was old, and his sight was gone. Naturally, he could not discern between the two boys. Normally, the practice was that the oldest child is supposed to get the blessing. To bestow that, the person giving the blessing would place their right hand on the eldest. Joseph had placed his sons correctly before his aging father according to tradition but at the last minute, Jacob crossed his hands giving the younger son the firstborn's blessing. That would make a difference. Despite Joseph's objections, Jacob proceeded to bless Ephraim the younger, believing it was what God desired. Once the impartation happened, it could not be undone. Something was transferred. The Spirit of God was on the old man to impart grace and transmit a spiritual destiny to his grandsons.

This is a principle of God that has not expired. It is still very much applicable for us today. While this may be new to some, and there may be some wrestling with this reality, impartation from one life to another is a kingdom phenomenon. This is an easier process when the recipient is open to receive what God has for them, and is willing to be discipled.

This impartation may look like a formal laying on of hands, like we see in the Scriptures, where both parties are aware of a tangible transfer. Or it may also be something you "catch" in the atmosphere, knowingly or unknowingly, by simply availing yourself to the people of God. When God gets His goods to you, He does not merely provide it in your private prayer time. Often, He uses other people as a delivery system.

Why is this? Why does God use *people* to disciple people? For one, I believe it is easy for someone to say they follow Jesus and not man when, in reality they don't follow the Jesus of the Bible either. Imagine Jesus taking a whip to the church because someone missed a prayer meeting or goofed off during church service like He did in the temple? If I did that, no one would come back to church. The need to be discipled by another person is not to lift up egos, man, or personalities, but because somebody has to animate this walk with God for us. Somebody has to live that surrendered life out, showing that it can be done. If a man or woman of God is not walking it out in front of us, often we are just chasing a carrot in front of us that we will never catch. Being connected with *other* disciples reminds us of what's possible and grafts us into the community God's designed for us. It is the very reason Paul said to follow him as he followed Christ (see 1 Corinthians 11:1). This is the secret of making disciples.

Today, we need role models of what a man or woman of God looks like. When I got saved, I had an awesome role model. This man let me live in his garage and modeled the Word of God to me. When I looked at him, I saw a true, authentic man of God and it gave me hope that this thing was real. I understood that the Bible was not just a story book or something we do on Sundays, but a way of life that can be lived out.

I learned that I can be what Jesus wants me to be—a genuine man of God. I sat under a man who taught me this by his life. He did not just tell me to do something I was not doing, but he lived it out. He was building in me what he had first built in himself. People do not spread the disease they do not have. Life begets life. He imparted to me what had first been realized in himself. He showed me a lifestyle that I was able to follow. I was able to see a blueprint. His life was an instruction manual for me.

Brothers and sisters, too many of God's people in the world today are not leaving blueprints for others to see. Paul, in his ministry pursuits, was known for this sort of blueprinting. When speaking on impartation and lifestyle to the Thessalonians, he said, "So, affectionately longing for you, we were well pleased to impart to you not only the gospel of God, but also our own lives, because you had become dear to us" (1 Thessalonians 2:8 NKJV).

Here the word *impart* implies that it was not just a desire to give head knowledge or information, but to give the gospel, the very thing that God had gifted to change our lives. When I was living out of the garage and soaking up what the man of God was modeling, I was seeing the gospel *and* a life imparted to me. This matters, not just because I am a pastor, but because I now disciple other men. I'm conscious of the fact the steps I take are going to be seen as steps to follow in. It's no light matter. Other things should not eat up priority in my life. If I do not take my walk with God seriously I will fail those who look to me as their leader. Before I am a pastor, I am a disciple. We are all to be disciples before we are anything else. This is why realizing we leave behind a trail of blueprints with our lifestyle is not just critical to pastors and leaders. We all need a healthy dose of revelation in this area. As believers, our lives are on display, and those around us are on the witness stand. What are they seeing, and what are they duplicating?

It should be clear by now that impartation is not merely some mystical injection of grace that performs some unknown role in our spiritual lives. It is the practical function of a mentor to a disciple. It is the onramp for giving the heart of God to other people. It is the process of transferring the reality of what God has done for you to someone else. As we alluded to earlier, it's not about what's *taught* but what's *caught*. The reality is, though, we only catch what we have a net for. Hunger is our net. Humility is our net. Commitment is our net. These things allow us to grab something beyond mere words. We are able to grab the spirit and heart behind what's being said.

Impartation and Transition

It's not uncommon in the Bible to see impartations occurring just before big transition. It's as if God is filling our tank before a big trip. Whether it's Joshua receiving an impartation from Moses before stepping into new heights of leadership or Paul and Barnabas having hands laid on them before being sent out. Impartation can empower us to do what we could not do otherwise. It's a transmission of grace that gives us the fuel to go where we could not on our own.

In fact, I never wished to come to Kansas City to pastor. Like I mentioned prior, I was set on planting a church in Chicago. Yet I had received a gracious impartation from a leader in my life, and that impartation enabled me to make the difficult move, commit to living for God and start pastoring a church in a city I knew nothing about. Every church established by God is led by people who felt His call on their lives. There are some great men and women of God ministering the gospel, but they didn't step into that callings all by themselves. Somehow, someway, somebody impacted them. Somebody stirred and challenged them. Whether conscious or unconscious, an impartation was released.

Transition usually requires vision. It takes a new lens

through which we see the world. Impartation is often the means by which God gets this vision to us. In fact, the very motivation of a disciple is not just to make heaven and avoid hell. It is to catch a vision—not a vision of success, wealth, or being a TV star—but a vision of God's harvest and kingdom. A true disciple acquires this vision through impartation, and then transfers this vision onto those they disciple. Once the disciple grabs the vision—a life is changed forever. Solomon wrote, "Where there is no vision the people perish but he that keeps the law happy is he" (Proverbs 29:18 KJV).

I have this old, dusty banner with this very scripture that I have kept throughout my years of ministry. It has hung in every church building we have occupied as a reminder to keep the vision alive. We pointed at that banner while we preached, talked, and sang about it. We have always fought to keep a kingdom vision. When the vision is lost, somebody perishes. Somebody else loses the call of God over their life. Disobedience to the vision affects others, reminding us that it's not all about us.

No one just wakes up and becomes a disciple. There is nothing automatic about it. With the call comes the decision for us to drop our nets and follow Jesus. Discipleship looks like impartation. It looks like somebody walking the walk who is able to teach those steps to somebody else. The guiding playbook along the way is the Word of God, and the referee who keeps the integrity between the two and facilitates growth is the Holy Spirit. The mutual exchange of grace is carried out by the Spirit of God. You cannot teach at length on the value of impartation without including the reality of the Holy Spirit. He is the One who breathes on the truths that we've had imparted. He is the One who empowers us to carry out the lifestyle we have seen modeled.

At the start of the book of Acts, Jesus gave some parting instruction to His disciples. He said, "But you shall receive power when the Holy Spirit has come upon you; and you shall be witnesses to Me in Jerusalem, and in all Judea and Samaria, and to the end of the earth" (Acts 1:8 NKJV).

The Holy Ghost was given to empower us to go into the world to preach the gospel and disciple others. This empowerment was not meant for us to argue theologies or sit in sanitized buildings debating nonsense. The Bible says in the second chapter of Acts that there was a visible flame that came on the heads of everyone that was praying in the upper room. With that endowment, the receivers were to start a fire and spread it all over the world, like a fire out of control, one brush igniting another.

Keep in mind, though, that this flame will not stay lit on its own. What has been imparted must be stewarded. We must kindle it and keep it burning. The Bible instructs that we ought to work out our own salvation with fear and trembling (see Philippians 2:12). We cannot blame others when our fire goes out, and we cannot shift responsibility to others for our lack of progress. My personal state is to be stewarded by me, ultimately. We are the keeper of our own soul and responsible for our own walk. If the fire on our heads, so to speak, goes out—we can't blame the rain.

We should blame ourselves for walking into it. Learn to put yourself in places that fuel your fire.

Recently, a leader in my church told me that he and his disciples had more passion and fire when they evangelized and followed up on people than when they did nothing. Why is that? Maybe it is because when we are actually doing the will of God, the Holy Spirit gets right in the middle and fuels the excitement.

In the modern church, we have reduced scriptures in Acts to tongue-talking doctrine or an emphasis on gifts (which have their place) but the reality is, the Spirit empowers us to reach the world and witness for Jesus. Sharing our faith, making disciples, remaining faithful—these things are not optional. Even amidst personal difficulty, the Spirit empowers us to hear and obey.

Many obstacles will try to keep us from fulfilling our calling. Humanity has never been short on detours. Rain will come to douse the flame that's been put in you. Yet our call is to allow the Spirit to impart power to us and surmount the difficulties no matter the cost. This swipes the excuses out from under us. What happened to us in our past should not be the reason we cannot live for God. No, my friend, this is like a marriage covenant where we say we are in this union in sickness or in health, and for better or for worse.

Consider the following scripture: "My sheep listen to my voice; I know them, and they follow me" (John 10:27 NLT). Notice, God's sheep not only listen but follow. They don't merely gather information on a Sunday, but they take steps according to what they heard and live it out on Monday. They cling to the Spirit's guidance and understand delegated authority. This is a hardcore passion that should be the fire of our lives. Jesus breathed upon His disciples in John 20 to receive the Holy Spirit. This was not some empty ritual but a spiritual grace that He also wants to bestow on us today. There is a fire to be imparted, and your heart is the receiver.

Not only do we receive the impartation of fire, but we somehow become it. The Bible says, "And of the angels He says: 'Who makes His angels spirits and His ministers a flame of fire'" (Hebrews 1:7 NKJV). This is for you and I. We, as His ministers, *are* a flame of fire. There was no such thing as a licensed, ordained preacher in the Bible. Peter was not a licensed ordained "501C-3 minister," elected by a board of directors or situated on a deacon board. He was purely and simply plucked out of his old ways by Jesus and placed into the flaming reality of passion and hardcore outreach. Every disciple of Christ, you and I included, is called to go into all the world and make disciples. We are called to go and preach the gospel and be, not just a minister, but an actual flame of fire.

I have always had this dream: imagine if every person of the thousands of people that flock to our churches on Sundays would just witness to one person during the week. If just half of those people lead one person to the Lord, what a harvest that would be! The Word of God does not come back void. The problem is not that God does not want to use us to build His kingdom, the problem is God's people do not want to be used. Most of the church world is content to sing the songs, listen to an inspirational message, and drop off an offering.

Honestly, I do not care if you are a Baptist, Methodist, Lutheran, Pentecostal or Assemblies of God, because back in the day, it was common for everyone to have church in the middle of the week. The reason why they don't do this anymore is because people don't want to. I have been a pastor since 1993, and I have heard it all. I can tell you all the excuses people come up with to avoid church. People would rather be somewhere else other than church, and you know your heart is going to follow the things you treasure. Many have chosen to isolate themselves and pull away when they should be running into the presence of God and His people.

In fact, isolation is a warning that someone has lost their fire. This person is the last person to arrive at church and the first one to leave. Their desire to be around passionate people of God diminishes. They avoid leadership because they are afraid that they will ask the big question, which is, *How are you?*

Because they get convicted around people that are on fire, they usually hang around other people that have lost theirs. Condemnation, embarrassment, and shame begins to come in, and they become fearful to witness. They become ashamed of radical praise, feeling unworthy to clap or lift their hands.

The reason for this loss of passion is because they are in a drained condition. No longer are they refueled in prayer and the Word of God. Spiritual warfare has raged, and battle after battle brought them to this place. Weariness begins to set in, accompanied by burnout.

Passion is critical for the supernatural to take place. It is going to take some boldness for us to lay hands on people and to release a prophetic word from God. We need passion if we are going to fulfill our ministry. And the good news is that if we have lost our passion for God it can be recaptured! If you have experienced impartation in the past and lost that transmission, you can get it back. Humbly submit yourself to the Lord and those He places over you. Readjust the antennas of your spirit until you begin picking up a signal again. If God did it for you once, He will do it again. Where He is wanting to take you is beyond what you are capable of in the present. Learn to lean into the impartations of Heaven, and gain the fuel you need for the ride.

CHAPTER EIGHT

SANCTIFIED VIOLENCE

IF YOU HAVEN'T already, it's time to fire apathy in your life. Evict double mindedness, and violently push back against slothfulness. The time for passivity is over. We are called to be untamed lions, incapable of becoming domesticated house cats! Consider this early New Testament passage: "And from the days of John the Baptist until now the kingdom of heaven suffers violence, and the violent take it by force" (Matthew 11:12 NKJV).

It's simple; the kingdom is taken and experienced, not by the passive, but by those with a violent, passionate, hardcore, steady, fierce flame in their souls. The weak-willed bench-riders will not see a fraction of the kingdom that the hardcore players on the court will experience.

God always has an agenda. He is the great designer, the architect of life, meaning He is the opposite of aimless. In the same way that He has an agenda for us, He had a specific agenda for Israel, and needed someone to take initiative during the reign of King Ahab. Who was the guy for the job? Our friend Elijah from chapter three.

Elijah was unique in that he had no special or unique talent. In fact, James says, "Elijah was a man with a nature like ours, and he prayed earnestly that it would not rain; and it did not rain on the land for three years and six months" (James 5:17 NKJV). He had no governmental position. He did not attend the school of the prophets. In fact, it's possible that he was not even formally recognized as a prophet during his lifetime. God simply made him one. He prayed that it wouldn't rain, and it did not for almost four years. Did he curry some special favor with God to pull this off? Nope. His nature was like ours. He was simply a righteous man with fervent prayers.

In fact, when you take a peek at the original meaning of the passage in Greek, having a "nature like ours" means he had *emotions* like us. He was riddled with the same frailties as us, and we know he dealt with doubt just like we do at times. As a matter of fact, right after the showdown and exhibition of power on Mount Carmel, he was running and hiding from Jezebel. The same guy who confidently faced the false prophets and had them violently killed, was now hiding in fear of the King's wife. The Bible records, "And Ahab told Jezebel all that Elijah had done, also how he had executed all the prophets with the sword. Then Jezebel sent a messenger to Elijah, saying, 'So let the gods do to me, and more also, if I do not make your life as the life of one of them by tomorrow about this time.' And when he saw that, he arose and ran for his life" (1 Kings 19:1-3 NKJV). Just because he ran from Jezebel does not mean he was no longer God's man. Yes, Elijah may have gone through his ups and downs, but he did not quit. King Ahab and Jezebel both wanted to kill him, but that did not deter Elijah from issuing orders to Ahab in the midst of all of the turmoil. In fact, even before the showdown he had put Ahab in his place, in a heated exchange: "Then it happened, when Ahab saw Elijah, that Ahab said to him, 'Is that you, O troubler of Israel?' And he answered, 'I have not troubled Israel, but you and your father's house have, in that you have forsaken the commandments of the LORD and have followed the Baals'" (1 Kings 18:17-18 NKJV).

This story unfolds during one of the darkest hours of Israel's history. Baal worship had crept in and dominated the spiritual environment, and it was fully endorsed by King Ahab, who had allowed the worship of this false god to come in via his wife. When Jezebel had the prophets of God executed, she wasn't merely pushing back on another religion, she was standing against God's ordained spiritual leadership for the nation. She was attempting to tear down a rich heritage. The worship of Baal was not only idolatrous but went against everything God had set up for His people from long before Jezebel ever existed. The implications of this idolatry were extreme, leading to famine and drought ravaging the land.

Sadly, the people of Israel did not seem to care nor were they even trying to do anything about it. We have no record of the people crying out to God and repenting because of the famine, drought, or the execution of the prophets by an evil woman. Beyond that, there is zero record of them standing up to the false religion or calling out bad teaching. They were just going with the flow of the culture, doing what everyone else was doing.

They began to take life as it came and thought that nothing could be done about it. Their approach was, *Why get all uptight about it? Whatever will be, will be.* They did not want to wait on God, and heaven forbid they rock the boat! In an attempt at avoiding trouble, they resigned themselves to being quiet, small-minded believers (the term *believers* used loosely).

Elijah's obedience stood out in strong contrast to the king's rebellion and the rebellion of the people who followed suit. Timidity was nowhere in his heart. He approached and confronted the king boldly, without apology. While he had no legal right to do so, he had the right and the authority God put into his heart which trumped all else. Of course, as we read, the king saw Elijah as a mortal enemy and blamed his prayer to cut off rain. Elijah was the *troubler* of Israel in the King's eyes, yet he was the champion of Israel in God's.

Paraphrasing Elijah's response, he said: *"I didn't trouble anybody. You did. You did because you and your father led the people of God the wrong way and that is why this nation is in a mess."* This was an aggressive man! Just give me five strong men like that. Give me five women of God with this kind of boldness and watch the world shake. God can do more with a handful of fiery disciples than an entire army of passive church-goers who are afraid to take a stand.

Make Up Your Mind

Israel splitting loyalty between God and Baal is no isolated incident. Many so-called Christians today have divided their loyalty between God and the flesh, which ultimately is not loyalty at all. They sing songs to Jesus while moonlighting for the enemy. Thinking they cannot overcome their sin, they begin to compromise. They falter between two positions; they are up one day, and down the next. I am not talking about being perfectionists or taking a legalistic approach to the kingdom of God. What I am referring to is an issue of the heart. Today, we care plenty about Jesus and His business, but tomorrow is another story. Today, we want to get a hold of God, but tomorrow we couldn't care less. This is the faltering that God wills to wipe out.

Some just don't see the value of choosing full fidelity to God. "What's the big deal?" they might ask. Maybe they haven't seen the full measure of consequences. Perhaps they tried to kick a bad habit, and it didn't work so they've become content in compromise. Regardless, this lukewarm middle is no place to be, and it was when Israel found themselves there that Elijah burst on the scene. It's worth noting *who* Elijah addresses in his proclamations. The Bible says that judgment begins at the house of God first (see 1 Peter 4:17). Similarly, when Elijah appeared, he did not speak to the people of Baal or the false prophets. He looked directly at God's people and asked, "How long will you falter between two opinions? Make up your mind. Either God is God or follow this false god" (see 1 Kings 18:21).

Interestingly, when he put them on blast, they did not even say a word. As a pastor, I have been in situations where I've had to confront people with questions like, "What's going on in your life?" Often, they do not have a response. Sometimes their silence is saying everything. This is the hellish spirit of apathy that we live in today, and it is running rampant. Many of God's people have become bogged down with apathy. The very heartbeat of this book is the antithesis of apathy.

Being *apathetic* means a person has become passive, laidback, and unconcerned about what is happening to their nation, family, job, and personal life. As born-again Christians we can never afford to be apathetic when it comes to living according to what the Bible teaches. If we are going to see the kingdom of God grow and advance we cannot adopt a passive mindset. God cannot use the apathetic because the apathetic are unproductive. They are starved of motivation, and they are prone to procrastination. Nowhere in the Bible was anything ever done through somebody who was passive about their situation. When we shed apathy we become immune to faltering between two opinions.

Elijah fought the spirit of apathy and challenged Israel by proving plainly who the true God was. He showed them the bottom line. Unafraid, he forced the Israelites to decide to either go for God or to serve Baal as we read prior. Know that Elijah's question to Israel, *"How long will you falter be-*

tween two opinions?" is also God's question to us. How long will we falter in these specific areas of our lives? How long will we exist between two opinions?

Often, faltering can be traced to a *but* in our minds. I really want to sacrifice and get a hold of God, *but*; I really want to do ministry, *but*; I really want to fulfill my destiny, *but*. The reason the Israelites were faltering was because they feared God (having seen the results of the drought) but also wanted the favor of the king, so they tolerated Baal. They understood the judgment of God, so they did not want to totally back-slide, but they also wanted the benefits that came from serving Baal. They were caught in the middle. Believers today do that too, by playing both sides of the fence. Serving God but seeing Baal on the side.

What are we tolerating instead of overcoming? Are there habits, sins, or situations that we have stopped trying to overcome, and instead, we simply tolerate? Are there areas in our lives that need attention, but we have given up trying? Have we stopped fighting to develop necessary disciplines? God may be dealing with us about obedience issues, but instead of surrendering to conviction, we have calculated the price and figured it to be too high. As a result, the middle seems safer and less costly. This, my friends, is deception. The middle is not safer—the middle is where the believer goes to be eaten alive.

We are called to overcome and not merely *tolerate* the things of this world. From the start God gave Adam dominion and commissioned him to "subdue the earth" (see Genesis 1:28). We have come to a decision point, where a divided heart cannot stand. Elijah demanded a definite decision. A choice was presented, and should they refuse to make that choice, the choice would be made for them. Had Elijah not presented the options, I personally believe Israel would have gone after Baal whole-heartedly, and the nation would be lost. The decision point was not a one-time occurrence, though, as Joshua had also expressed similar challenges, saying, "Choose you this day whom you will serve. As for me and my house we will serve the Lord" (Joshua 24:15 PARA).

Later in the New Testament, Jesus was direct with similar sentiments, saying to Laodicea, "I know your works. I know you are neither cold nor hot…so then, because you are lukewarm, and neither cold nor hot, I will vomit you out of my mouth" (Revelation 3:15-16 NKJV).

Bear in mind, He was speaking to an actual church of New Testament believers, a people under the covenant of grace. I believe, too, that Jesus is saying these very words to the church today. The message that was seen in the time of Elijah: *How long are you going to exist in the middle?*

There is a popular story of a man who experienced a true God dream. In the dream he was straddling a fence. As he looked, he saw Jesus on one side of the fence and Satan on the other. He knew he was faced with a decision but refused to make one. Staying on the fence, the decision was made for him when suddenly Jesus disappeared and he was left with the enemy.

Troubled, he said to Satan, "Wait, I did not choose you. I chose the fence."

Satan then laughed and said, "I own the fence."

The truth is, being neutral in the spiritual realm is just not possible. Jesus said, "You are either for me or you are against me" (Matthew 12:30 NKJV). When we choose the fence, we are not choosing some neutral middle. We are choosing the enemy's camp.

I Sought for a Man

It can be difficult to find Christians that are bold in what they believe. Many seem to think that a Christian is supposed to be some sort of softie, and so our life approach tends to reflect that mentality. When Israel was coming under judgment for false worship, the people who grabbed a hold of the horns of the altar found refuge. God needs people today who will get a hold of the horns of the altar and not let go. He needs people who violently push past the noise to get to where God wants them to be.

Our going *all out* for Jesus should be without conditions. We will serve Him just as hard without a job as we do with one. With or without money we will go for God, and not let the things of this world dictate our joy or victory.

Where are the real men and women of God, today?

In 16th century Scotland, Mary Queen of Scots said, "I fear the prayers of John Knox more than all the assembled armies of Europe." John's prayers scared the queen because she had seen the results of those prayers and how strongly John expressed his faith during that period in history. People will recognize a man or woman of God especially if the power of God is demonstrated in their lives. That is why

Ahab dared not disobey Elijah's commands. If Elijah had not prayed for rain, the famine would have continued.

Even Herod had reason to fear when he heard about Jesus' ministry and boldness. He was afraid that John the Baptist, whom he had put to death, had come back to life. Why? Because John the Baptist was crazy aggressive in delivering the Word of the Lord. While locked up in chains, John called Herod an adulterer because Herod had married his brother's wife. John reminded the King that he was going to stand before God and answer for that decision. When Herod heard that a man was moving in power, as John the Baptist had, he thought that John was back from the dead.

Will we carry out a lifestyle that creates this sort of radical reputation? The spirit of apathy would like our answer to be *no*. We've all felt this at times. How do we know if we have it? Our minds will avoid being honest about where we are in life and in our walk with God. Instead of pressing towards the goal or forcefully taking our walk with God to the next level, we settle. We start to believe that we cannot get victory over the struggle, so we set up camp in compromise and stay there. If you feel like there is no use trying anymore, realize there is! When you got saved, you entered a battle—a spiritual one, and the fight goes on.

Laziness never facilitates victory, so refuse to have any part in it. When life does not work out the way we planned, the temptation is to give up. Remember, Christianity is not a sprint, but a journey. You won't be some polished and perfected saint tomorrow—so have patience with yourself as you get back into the fight. That is why the Bible says that he who endures till the *end* shall be saved. So take the long view and stay the course over time—it'll be worth it.

One of the more high profile passages on the subject of intercession comes up in the life of Ezekiel when the Lord said, "So I sought for a man among them who would make a wall and stand in the gap before Me on behalf of the land, that I should not destroy it; but I found no one" (Ezekiel 22:30 NKJV).

It's a tragic verse, knowing God lacked a single individual with a heart to stand in the gap. God is always seeking men and women to do His will. He is looking for somebody to heal this world, our community, and our families. May the phrase "I found no one" never leave God's lips as long as we have breath in our lungs.

The fact is, there are people who will not make it to heaven if we do not fulfill God's plan for our lives. We may think we are inadequate to fulfill the call of God or that the impact will be trivial; however, according to Ezekiel, one man standing in the gap can save an entire nation.

Anything God has done on earth has been done by forceful people. The Bible trumpets this reality from beginning to end. David was aggressive against Goliath. Peter preached boldly on the day of Pentecost and 3,000 people got saved. Moses approached the pharaoh, a ruler that could have taken his life instantly, and declared, "God said: let my people go!" Esther stood before the king, pleading for the people. She went to the king unannounced, which was against the law to do so without being summoned (even as queen). It was bold, shocking, and courageous.

Daniel made a bold decision while serving King Darius who made a law forbidding anyone to pray to any god other than himself. Punishable by death, this new law did not deter Daniel from praying openly when he heard about it. He did not go hide in the closet to pray; he opened his window and prayed for all to see.

What about Shadrach, Meshach, and Abednego? When the music played as everyone's cue for bowing down to the golden statue, they did not bow. Even though they knew the penalty for disobeying the law was being thrown in the fiery furnace, they chose loyalty to God over their own lives.

Jesus did not shirk from His obedience to God either. He went into Jerusalem knowing that He was facing the cross. He knew what awaited Him. Paul the apostle also knew what awaited him when he was taking the gospel to different cities. In one city he was beaten. In another, he was stoned, left for dead and got up and went straight back into the city.

In all of these accounts, we can see that there were men and women who did not deviate from forcefully moving forward. Know that when you received Christ, you were given a new DNA. Your mode of operation now as a child of God is one of zeal and tenacity. The passive get duped, they get left behind, they find themselves under hell's heel. The violent, though, take the kingdom by force and reclaim the rightful territory of God—for themselves, for their families, their churches, and their nation.

CHAPTER NINE

TRUE TREASURE

A PARADIGM SHIFT occurred in America in the 1980's when the U.S. census put out a statement that said, "America knows more about itself than ever before." The data produced insight on quality of life, causes of death, birth, divorce, crime, eating habits, and so on. With the rollout of this information, we knew ourselves frontwards and backwards.

The problem is, the world's solutions have not kept people's lives from falling apart. We may have more information about people, things, and circumstances, but this doesn't mean we have presented the right solutions to the problems we see. In many ways, we have gained head knowledge but lost our understanding of the value of people along the way.

Our battle is to fight to see people give their lives to Jesus Christ so that they will miss hell and gain heaven, and come to know the same Lord that has paid the price for their new destination. Followers of Jesus recognize that they are part of an army with this mission. Our lives become not our own but the Lord's and are to be used for the eternal salvation of others.

The Apostle Paul, in his epistles to the Corinthian church, reminded them of how much he had given of himself on their behalf. This was not just him, though. He said, "Imitate me just as I also imitate Christ" (1 Corinthians 11:1 NKJV). There were other leaders and believers who were a part of his team that were giving their lives for the spreading of the gospel, too. Many believers feel like they have been spent for kingdom purposes. Some have been spent physically and emotionally as well. Beyond that, there are those who take time off of work to do kingdom business, and it costs them financially.

One might ask, *Are Christians supposed to work this hard?* We read about some who give their lives for certain causes and purposes—folks do it all the time. Some go on hunger strikes, set up protests, and do all kinds of things to draw attention to their cause. I remember in the 1970's when a Buddhist monk burned his body as a living sacrifice in protest of the Vietnam War. All kinds of people have made radical sacrifices, even with their lives, for causes and purposes. Sadly, for some, they made the ultimate sacrifice but died on the wrong battlefield.

The fact is, we *are* called to work this hard for Jesus Christ. We are called to make massive sacrifices. This does not mean we burn out and neglect rest. It does not mean that we forget our families to attempt to save the world on the mission field. It *does* mean that we spend ourselves within the priority system God has given us, leaving nothing left in the cup at the end of the day. The glory of God is ready to be released in the earth, and your life lived in radical obedience is the spout.

Jesus Saw Value

> "Therefore, whether you eat or drink, or whatever you do, do all to the glory of God. Give no offense, either to the Jews or to the Greeks or to the church of God, just as I also please all men in all things, not seeking my own profit, but the profit of many, that they may be saved." (1 Corinthians 10:31-33 NKJV)

The answer to the problems of this world is not in our government or education. The real answer is in Jesus' claim that He is the Way, the Truth, and the Life (see John 14:6). You cannot catch this revelation from a human vantage point. We have to go beyond our earthly lens and look with the eyes of God, seeing His answers as the absolute truth for our world. This view provides us with a proper evaluation of people.

It is true that politicians, entertainers, movie stars, sports figures, and other celebrities are seen and thought of as more valuable in society because of their clout, fame, money, and talent. We look up to them, and if such people were to walk in a room, many of us would get nervous.

We might even feel that everyone else is less valuable than them, but in God's eyes, all people are equally valuable. No matter their social or financial standings; no matter their level of stardom or lack thereof, people are valued the same. Christ on the cross was the ultimate declaration that humanity is valued equally and fully by God.

The Bible destroys the world's measuring stick for human value. Apart from the gospel, we never get a true perspective on humanity, so we must see through the eyes of Jesus. The Bible shows that God knows all men. Seeing others through the eyes of God instead of our own impacts perception, which impacts action. Salvation gives us new eyes. I have not looked at life and people the same way since I gave myself to Jesus.

Jesus, the King of Kings, and the Lord of Lords does not need anything, yet the Bible says that He left heaven, His kingdom, His richness and became poor for our sake (2 Corinthians 8:9). Paul was stating that the Lord is the proprietor of all things, the possessor of Heaven and earth. When He came to earth as a man, He became as one that is a beggar, having nothing compared to what He had in Heaven. Jesus bankrupted Himself for souls. This goes against everything the culture teaches you.

We can only understand the value of people when we first understand the price that was paid for our salvation. The Gospel of John revealed the price of Jesus' incarnation when it stated that the Word became flesh and dwelt among us (see John 1:14). He paid a price by simply leaving Heaven and paid a price in the ministry by relentlessly spending Himself to heal the deaf, dumb, and blind. Several times according to the gospels, Jesus looked up to Heaven and sighed, even weeping with compassion because He saw the great need of the people. He did not come seeking out the rich and famous nor the most popular people in the world. He sought out the least popular: the prostitutes, tax collectors, fishermen, and the blind. He sought out those rejected by society. He found value in the unseen people whom others walked over in the streets.

On one such occasion, Jesus crossed the sea for His next assignment, which was a man who had been totally alienated from society—some might argue for good reason. He spent his time dwelling in graveyards and cutting himself with rocks. However, this did not keep Jesus from interacting with him. The scripture records, "And when He had come out of the boat, immediately there met Him out of the tombs a man with an unclean spirit" (Mark 5:2 NKJV).

This was not an ordinary man nor were the circumstances ordinary. He was possessed by a legion of demons. The people of the city were scared of him, so they tried to restrain him with chains. He howled at night and was known for self-harm. Just prior to this, Jesus had crossed the Sea of Galilee in the midst of a storm that almost wrecked the ship, causing His disciples to fear for their lives, yet a divine appointment was waiting for them. This man, who by today's standards, was a lunatic, happened to be that divine appointment. Jesus delivered the man, restored him to his right mind, and showed him great compassion.

Why single out this story on human value over the

many others in Scripture? Because Jesus told His disciples to cross over the Sea of Galilee where they faced a storm, and their focus shifted to the circumstances. They were concerned about the storm and the waves. They feared for their own lives. When they got their eyes off of the missions and on to the mess, their authority had been castrated. Jesus' concern however, in spite of the storm, was for a demon possessed man; a single soul, waiting on the other side. This pattern is a regular occurrence today. When storms hit our lives, we often immediately begin to think of ourselves and totally forget about lost souls. Yet souls are the very reason for the ultimate price paid at Calvary and should not be forgotten, in good times or in bad.

Souls are not saved by joining a church. Souls are not saved by reading self-help. Souls are saved by the proclamation and acceptance of the price for redemption—which was the precious blood of Jesus. It cost God nothing to create this beautiful world as He simply spoke it into being. But it cost Him the death of His Son to save and restore helpless people like you and me.

One can't help but be convicted when looking at the life of Paul. He said he had become all things to all men in order to save some (1 Corinthians 9:22). He was not prejudiced. He just wanted souls and lived with that very burden. This kind of thinking challenges us today because we have turned Christianity and our churches into spiritual social self-help groups. We come to church today to better ourselves and our families. Don't get me wrong, there are benefits in the kingdom for our families, marriages, children, and so forth. Getting our homes in order does not come somewhere after missions, but here is a caution for us: we should not get so caught up in, "What's in it for me?" that we forget that Jesus commanded us to go into all the world and share our faith.

Let's not forget Paul's words: "Now it's up to you. Be on your toes—both for yourselves and your congregation of sheep. The Holy Spirit has put you in charge of these people—God's people they are—to guard and protect them. God himself thought they were worth dying for" (Acts 20:28 MSG).

The church is not a society of people to merely admire Christ, Christian ethics and ideals, but it has been purchased by Jesus' own blood. He found worth in people that set the price of their salvation so high, the only payment was the innocent blood of God. Let this appraisal be a driving force.

Are You Currency?

Impressive people are not more valuable. Unimpressive people are not less valuable. Their status or lack thereof is not the measurement of worth, and our valuation of others is not based on how they benefit us or how much they could potentially do on our behalf. Our valuation is based solely on the love of God displayed at Calvary. Paul said, "Because of this decision we don't evaluate people by what they have or how they look. We looked at the Messiah that way once and got it all wrong, as you know. We certainly don't look at him that way anymore" (2 Corinthians 5:16 MSG).

Our church, *The Cure*, is a unique one in that we prayed, "Lord give us those that nobody else wants." Through the years God has answered. During altar calls in our services, I have looked out and seen people from every walk of life responding to God; the rich, the poor, the known, and the unknown alike. People are coming forward looking for hope. They heard that God loves, values, and cares for them, and that rare message finds a home in their hearts and, somehow, by an act of grace, He wooed them and brought them in. Make no mistake, Jesus is the one that saves people. We have not paid for their redemption; we are just the ones who tell them about their new balance in the sight of God.

The world's system generally looks to give when that giving will be reciprocated. Our system is different. When the world asks, "What's in it for me?" the believer drops the self-serving front and simply pours out. It's been said that the earthly trinity is me, myself, and I. We like generosity when it's either easy or has guaranteed reciprocation. We make choices as if going to a yard sale, meaning, we want something for cheap or free. If we are not careful, this philosophy creeps into our hearts as servants of Jesus, yet God has called us to a radical new outlook in life where we love even when we are not loved in return. We start to care about people whom we don't know and perhaps have nothing in common with. The heart of God in ours enables us to pull this off.

"I'd be most happy to empty my pockets and even mortgage my life for your good. So how does it happen that the more I love you the less I'm loved." (2 Corinthians 12:15 MSG)

Paul was not speaking just about finances here. He was referring to giving his actual life for the benefit of others. See, our lives are a currency for the kingdom to be spent as God sees fit. How have you been spending yourself? Our lives are a currency just like the currency in our wallets or in our bank accounts. Once we give our lives to Jesus, they no longer belong to us. You do not own the title deed to your life; the One who paid for it does.

Paul describes this *spending* "as sorrowful, yet always rejoicing; as poor, yet making many rich; as having nothing, and yet possessing all things" (2 Corinthians 6:10 NKJV). Again, he was not alluding to his financial state. He was describing an exchange, wherein he was bankrupting himself to make others rich in Christ. He recognized that his energies, influences, money, skills, strength, and time, are all marketable. He was not looking for any earthly return but a heavenly reward. What would happen if we adopted this mentality and saw our time and effort as a debit card, drawing on the resources God has given us? It would call us to action, knowing that when the curtain closes on this life, we cannot take our account balance with us. We have one chance to spend in this window called life.

Paul knew his life was a gift to be spent and not a resource to be hoarded. This should be the same for us. Being stingy is not an admirable character trait. You may notice stingy people at the restaurant when the bill comes, yet somehow, they *always* wind up in the bathroom at that time, letting someone else pick up the check. We should be the ones eager for the check, so to speak. We ought to be the ones eager to release our finite lives as agents of blessing to those around us.

To swing this sort of thinking and behavior, we have reset our value system. The old value system needs to be nuked and replaced with a biblical one. Paul gives us a clue in his letter to the Philippians when he said, "Yet indeed I also count all things loss for the excellence of the knowledge of Christ Jesus my Lord, for whom I have suffered the loss of all things, and count them as rubbish, that I may gain Christ" (Philippians 3:8 NKJV).

Rubbish in the Greek means *dung*, or *poo*. Why take this approach? Because it's hard to covet dung. You will never abdicate generosity because you are busy hoarding and idolizing things you see as dung. This proper view of our *stuff* lets us see that titles, accolades, cash balances, and possessions matter little in light of eternity. This is obviously not rational to blow up a budget or forget sound principles of stewardship. This is, rather, a call to reset how we view the spending column of our lives. This is a call to pluck possessions off of the pedestal.

The failure to see this truth is nothing new. Scripture reveals several accounts of this very thing. In Matthew 25, for example, three men were given talents. One was given five talents, one was given two, and another one was given one talent. The man with just one talent would not invest it for the master's profit if it was not going to profit him. Self-interest always contradicts the Spirit of Christ, and it insults God. The master in this parable minced no words calling him a wicked and lazy servant.

In the parable of the rich fool in Luke 12:20, we see that Jesus was not condemning the man for having money. There were rich disciples and still are. The problem was the rich man was focused on his achievement of bigger things, and larger barns, but his life and his money were not the currency of the kingdom.

There is yet another story in the gospels of a woman who was a harlot. She came to see Jesus and with her she brought an alabaster box that was filled with costly perfume. The alabaster box was so expensive it cost about an entire year's worth of wages. Breaking the alabaster box, she anointed Jesus' feet with it and wept as she wiped them with her hair. This act was preparing and anointing Jesus for burial, but beyond that, it was a display of genuine worship. How much is a year's wages for the average person reading this book? What would it look like to pour out in this way? Would we view sacrificing for Christ as waste? Or would we realize that pouring out for His sake is just the opposite of waste. The truth is, there are no rewards for these other earthly pursuits we give our time to, but, for a life poured out to Jesus, there certainly are.

When we understand what Jesus has done for us, and how indebted to Him we are, viewing our lives as currency comes easy. Somehow, though, this is a far cry from American Christianity today. More prevalent here is the thinking, *What is the least amount of time we can commit to God and still call ourselves Christians?* Instead of going all out for Him, many think of what they can get away with and still go to Heaven.

Paul conveyed that he was in debt to God for life because he was on his way to hell and God spared him. His indebtedness to the Greeks, barbarians, to the wise and unwise did not mean that he owed them anything, but because he owed God for all His goodness, he was indebted to them as a result. Money was not what was owed here. No, Paul understood that because God loved these people, he too must love them the same way, and he lived his life on that hook. Paul did not count his life dear to himself. The objective of the kingdom of God is to gain such a mindset. Unfortunately, it has been lost on many. Rarely do Christians today share Paul's stance. It is more common to find believers who do not feel indebted to anyone this way. More likely, they are mad at or embittered toward others, even other church-folk. They might blame other people for their problems or view them as an inconvenience. Christianity trumpets a different message. People are not a problem to avoid. People are runways for the love of God to land on. I am a debtor. I owe something. I have something on trust for these people. Paul was saying that *he* was a currency.

Years ago they began to remodel St. John's church in New York City. It cost them 20 million dollars for the roof alone and many years to complete the project. Some of the sculptors and stone masons came from Europe to work on the steeples and monuments. My wife and I saw this when we were in New York. Plenty of money, effort and energy went into building two religious-looking towers which, frankly, were not critical in protecting worshippers from the elements. The lives of God's people, to be spent for the kingdom, have infinitely greater value than those church towers.

Laying up for ourselves treasure in Heaven speaks to an eternal value system. Heaven's economy is different from our earthly banking system, for Heaven's economy treasures souls above all else. Caring for, pursuing, and rescuing souls is the root of our reward and the evidence of our impact.

Even churches that believe in and consistently preach about the value of people need to be careful. Stressing the importance of winning the world through evangelism and discipleship is not enough. The danger of this is that we may hear it so much that we become numb to it. Paul not only preached it but emphasized it with his action. It was not mere words for him. His *lifestyle* was the exclamation point at the end of the sentence. Your life is like a 100 dollar bill that you found. You can spend it how you wish. Let me encourage you, the rewards, the eternal impact, and the glorious blessing of pouring it out for the cause of Christ far surpass any temporary gain from self-centered living.

When Paul said, "I, too, try to please everyone in everything I do. I don't just do what is best for me; I do what is best for others so that many may be saved" (1 Corinthians 10:33 NLT), he was not isolating this lifestyle to apostles and pastors. It was a blueprint for all believers. The fallacy that preachers are called to a special place of devotion over the layman has been tolerated for too long. The clergy and the congregation may have differing duties and responsibilities, but we have the same call to be spent as the account holder sees fit.

Addicted to the Ministry

I was addicted to drugs at 14 years of age. The addiction was so bad that while my mom was in the kitchen cooking, I was in the restroom breaking up her diet pills to stick in my arm with a needle. Constantly looking for a high, I sold drugs, stole, and did whatever it took to feed the addiction. I sought after valium and cocaine and even hurt others to get them. I remember running home from school and sitting there shaking, waiting for a diabetic guy I knew to come over so that I could use one of his insulin needles. There was a point in my life when I could not look at a spoon without wanting to throw up because it made me think of drugs. I could not stop even if I wanted to, and I was to the point of harming myself. Thankfully, God radically saved me and turned my life around. My addictions were erased and replaced with better ones, godly ones.

> "I beseech you, brethren, (ye know the house of Stephanas, that it is the first fruits of Achaia, and that they have addicted themselves to the ministry of the saints)" (1 Corinthians 16:15 KJV).

Notice, the Word says they had *addicted* themselves to the ministry of the saints. This is the sanctified and commendable addiction. Being addicted means you could lose sleep over what you are addicted to. You will do whatever it takes to have it. You make sacrifices for it. These were regular disciples who could not get enough of doing stuff for people. They were hooked on serving.

When Jesus said, "Freely you have received, freely give" (Matthew 10:8 NKJV), He was saying that everything we receive from God is held in trust on the behalf of others. How is it that we freely receive and then complain about having to give our lives to others? Jesus said it is more blessed to give than to receive (see Acts 20:35 NKJV). Why settle for an inferior blessing? It is love for Jesus that gives us our burden for souls and addicts us to ministry.

I've been asked, "How can I get a burden for souls?" I've been told that I can be intense about the issue of souls. The answer is that as we love God, He gives us His affections. A love for Him leads to a love for the stuff He loves. So it's only natural that the God who loves the souls of humanity would impart that same love to those who seek His will. We cannot separate our love for God from our love for people. John said, "If someone says, 'I love God,' and hates his brother, he is a liar" (1 John 4:20).

Christians today can resemble Pharisees at times, talking about their knowledge of God, posting scriptures, sounding spiritual, but when it comes down to their actual lives—they are not checkbooks ready to be spent. They look more like vaults. The good they have to give is inaccessible. They spend more time criticizing and critiquing than spending their lives for the winning of souls.

Loving God and loving people will cause us to give money, talent, and time to what God finds valuable. Though this is a hard word for most because it goes against our very culture and nature, the rewards are great. Make no mistake about it, the life of a soul winner is not dry, lifeless and miserable. Just the opposite! The Scriptures say, "Yes, says the Spirit, they are blessed indeed, for they will rest from their hard work; for their good deeds follow them!" (Revelation 14:13 NLT).

Don't pour out hard work for a pastor or a religious organization. If you do, your reward will be limited to them. However, if you do it for the Lord, you will be rewarded *by* the Lord. Throw yourself at the work of God. Paul said, "If a man desires the position of a bishop, he desires a good work" (1 Timothy 3:1 NKJV). He hit the nail on the head here. If you are a pastor or leader, quit prolonging childish things! Why become so infatuated with mere fun and not the serious issues of the kingdom like souls and eternity?

Throw yourself into the work of the Master, being confident that nothing you do for Him is a waste of time. God desires for believers to be steadfast always, and to abound in the Word of God. Unfortunately, not just the world but even some believers today put down those who want to teach God's Word. Paul said this is to desire a good work. Ministry is not for the cool, calm, collected, or complacent. Ministry is for hardcore, loyal, steadfast, strong, and gritty people who don't fear giants but slay them. Don't let anyone tell you otherwise. God's Word is not to be locked in a vault but is to be fired from the canon of our lives.

Perhaps you've saved when you should have sowed. Maybe you've been conservative when you should have given freely. Many have kept to themselves when they were called to give of themselves. Let your pursuit of God birth in you the very desire of God, which is to draw all people to Himself. The influence of the church of Jesus is depending on people like you and I to begin making withdraws and spending who we are and what we have on those around us.

CHAPTER TEN

UNMATCHED ADVENTURE

SOME TIME AGO, I went out with a group to a local restaurant after a Red Rain concert, a Christian band from New Zealand. We were all sitting there talking when the waitress came over, a 22-year-old with a horrible attitude. In this particular restaurant, there were usually at least five area preachers there on any given Sunday night. The waitress, hearing the accent of the band members, asked where they were from.

"New Zealand," they replied.

"Wow! What are you doing in Kansas?" They explained and from there she started complaining and spewing negativity.

One of the band members interjected saying, "This is a pastor."

Glancing at me she retorted, "That's not a pastor. This guy looks like a pimp." We were still dressed for the concert from that night. Then she continued, "There are all kinds of pastors around here. He ain't no pastor."

I just sat there and let it settle in, realizing that this young woman was torn up. When she walked away, I told two of the guys with us that this lady was going to get saved. God had just spoken to me about it. They just looked at me, probably thinking, *What do you mean she is going to get saved?* She came back later, and I began to prophesy over her, saying, "One thing you hate, and why you're so angry and why you targeted your anger toward me at this table is because you are sick and tired of preachers coming in here, and they see you hurting, and yet, they won't even tell you that Jesus loves you, but they'll leave you a flyer at the table."

She looked at me, pulled a flyer out and said, "It just happened. I'm sick of this, they know I'm hurting." I began to pray for her, and she gave her life to Jesus.

Afterward, the band looked at me. The guitar player, with tears in his eyes, said, "Pastor, we travel all over the world, and we go out and eat with pastors all the time. I've never seen a pastor witness to somebody." That kind of rocked me when he said that. I said, "Dude, I'm better in the streets than I am in my own church."

The truth is, I had learned early on from the men of God that I observed and followed that believers share their faith with others, period. Our evangelism should have no off-button.

Life can be a wonderful adventure when put in God's hands. If people want to live a boring, mundane, and miserable life, they certainly can. We can all live a life where we just wake up, go to work, eat, go to sleep, and then do the same thing again the next day. But if anyone wants to live for God, then they need to let Him use their life to cast out demons, perform miracles, and see people give their hearts to Jesus. Our walk with God is far more exciting this way!

Don't Quit

Here is the reality: this adventurous outpouring is for the good times and the bad ones. Often, when people go through a hard time, they immediately become introspective and forget their call to make disciples and live a hardcore life of faith. I've heard people in my church look at me when things are good in my life and say, "Pastor, you don't have any problems."

First, this isn't true—I, like everyone else, deal with issues all the time. In fact, some of the worst things that have happened to me took place since getting saved, and I lived a pretty crummy life as a sinner. Somehow, by the grace of God, He did not allow me, nor did I allow myself, to let those things bring fear, stop me, take root, or cause me to quit. There were many times in my life when I had the opportunity to give in.

Years ago, I pastored our church for 11 months without a car. My wife took the bus with my son James to do the laundry and get groceries, even in the winter. There were times when I called up church members and asked if they could give me a ride to church so that I could preach for them. Add to that the loss of a child, being told by doctors that we would not be able to have kids again, and my wife being sick for years. We had so many people prophesy over us that we would have kids again, and it never happened. Those were some rough times for my family, but I did not quit. I decided not to give up because I kept certain things in my mind. The Bible says to count it all joy whenever trials and temptations come to us (see James 1:2).

Seeing the big picture has a way of keeping us from throwing in the towel. Souls are at stake, and there is a mission to fulfill. Preaching about not quitting, teaching it in Bible studies, or telling people in the hallway of a church is easy. It's another story, though, when we are the recipient of difficult situations, and everything in us wants to cave. We are good at giving advice to others, but living out that advice is another story.

Our entire spiritual lineage has been built, not on the lives of pansies and cowards, but on the blood of martyrs. We stand on the shoulders of those who didn't cave, even with their lives on the line. Paul was blinded by God in a vision, gave his life to Jesus, eventually went into the ministry, and experienced a series of setbacks and hardships. Nevertheless, he was instrumental in the propagation of the gospel to the Gentiles and eventually, modern Europe. Had he caved, the influence of the gospel would have been stifled.

Philip also preached the gospel to an Ethiopian who brought the gospel for the first time to Africa. Ethiopia today has a rich Christian history as a result, yet that started because a man of God was willing to be bold, despite an atmosphere that was not conducive to public ministry. The early church availed themselves to the leading of the Spirit and seized opportunities to witness for the gospel. In the process, many lost their lives. They had caught a vision from God, and it was simply stored their hearts. They did not end up on television, with mass acclaim, nor did they have five million followers on social media. They occupied the difficult position God gave them and were joyously sharing Christ, even up until the point of death. For example, Mathew suffered martyrdom in Ethiopia where he was killed with the sword; Mark died in Alexandria, Egypt where he was dragged by horses through the streets until he was dead. Luke was hung in Greece as a result of his tremendous preaching to the lost. John was boiled alive in a huge basin of oil during a wave of persecution. He was miraculously delivered and was then sentenced to the mines in an Isle of Patmos where he wrote the prophetic Book of Revelation.

 He was later freed to return as a bishop in modern-day Turkey. He was the only Apostle to die peacefully. Peter was crucified upside down on an X-shaped cross according to church tradition because he told his tormentors that he felt unworthy to die the same way as Jesus. James, the brother of Jesus, who was a leader of the church in Jerusalem, was thrown from the southeast Pinnacle of the Temple, a height of 100 feet, when he refused to deny his faith. When his persecutors discovered that he survived, they ran down and beat him to death with a club. This was the same Pinnacle where Jesus was taken by Satan during one of His temptations. James the son of Zebedee, whom Jesus called to a lifetime of ministry as a strong leader of the church, was ultimately beheaded in Jerusalem.

The Roman soldier who guarded James watched, fully amazed, as James defended his faith at his trial. Later the officer walked beside him to the place of execution, and overcome with conviction, he declared his new faith in Jesus and knelt beside James and accepted beheading as well. Bartholomew, also known as Nathaniel, was a missionary to Asia and present-day Turkey. He was whipped to death for preaching. Thomas was struck with a spear and died on one of his missionary trips, establishing a church in India. Jude, another brother of Jesus, was killed by arrows after refusing to deny Christ. Matthias, the one who replaced Judas Iscariot, was stoned and beheaded. Barnabas, who was one of the group of the 70 disciples, was stoned to death.

Paul the apostle was in prison and wrote many of the Epistles in the Bible during that time. Prior to that, he had traveled throughout the Roman Empire and taught many the foundations of Christianity. Eventually, Paul was tortured and then beheaded by the evil emperor Nero, in Rome. This was the same emperor that Paul urged believers to pray for and submit to, as he was the leader in AD 67.

Most Christians today do not possess such determination or attitude in regard to their faith. God help us! Paul's attitude was set on pleasing God, and he was not disobedient to the heavenly vision. He was determined to fight the good fight and to keep the faith. He pressed toward the mark of the prize of the high calling in Christ. His letter to Timothy before he died stated that he understood that he did not have it all together nor was he a perfect man.

We can view our lives soberly knowing that we do not have it all together, but we can still run strong for God and finish our race. As a pastor, I have to deal with things like anyone else. I deal with people and their emotions, besides my own. My life and marriage are not perfect, but it does not stop me. My desire is to finish my race knowing that I did not fight my leader, the church, and those that I pastor. When I finish I want to know that I fought the good fight—that I did not fight with politics or hold grudges. No matter the issue, I want to die saying that I was not disobedient to God's vision for my life.

Toward the end of Paul's life, he summarized his advice to a young minister, Timothy, by saying, "So, my son, throw yourself into this work for Christ. Pass on what you heard from me—the whole congregation saying Amen!—to reliable leaders who are competent to teach others. When the going gets rough, take it on the chin with the rest of us, the way Jesus did" (2 Timothy 2:1-7 MSG).

Where It Counts

Being hardcore disciples and making hardcore disciples is difficult if our home is not in order. We cannot export what we have not first carried out in the home. The movie *Radio* plays out an incredible storyline of a successful football coach who was admired and well liked by his community and school, but was a failure at home. He neglected his family and did not communicate well with them; meanwhile he poured his heart and soul into his football team.

Things changed when he decided to help a special-needs kid to integrate into society. People had made fun of the kid, including the football team. The coach tried to father him, but the kid was not received well by the football team, community, school, and even his own family. The decision to help the kid seemed like it was going to cost him his coaching career and more.

Eventually, a conversation with his daughter ensues with him apologizing for failing her as a father and describing how that failure had shaped his life. By recognizing it, he was not going to let that get the best of him, and he wanted to make a difference in the life of this one boy named Radio. His own failures in the home did not keep him from beginning again.

Do not be confused; family relationships can be messy, but we can face our failures, make changes and take up responsibility. Active parenting means we raise our kids in the admonition of the Lord. Allowing a child to be so wrapped up in everything else besides the things of God is not active parenting. If our kids are involved with sports to the degree that there's no time for God, the sport (or whatever activity it might be) has become a little god. Setting a home in order and creating disciples under the roof of our own homes may be the most valuable ministry we do. I would be remiss to not place some special emphasis on this reality.

Wrap-Up

Being a disciple of Christ is a message and a lifestyle that has been on my heart for several years. Admittedly, I am saddened to see the people of God not giving Him their absolute best—not out of legalistic obligation, but out of a loving desire to never forget God's Son and His suffering for us.

Christ hung, blood-drenched on the cross while mutilated flesh clung to His back. His beard was ripped from His face. He was spat upon and mocked. All this that we might be saved and restored to a right relationship with God.

It seems that in our modern era, the body of Christ has lost its zeal for God. It has lost that desire and fire. Our passion for God and the things of His kingdom can begin to waiver at times, for whatever reason. Life gets hard and we begin to grow cold towards Him.

Putting this book together did not come without much spiritual warfare. I began to question the Lord about why I felt so much resistance. He revealed that it was because I was going up against a territorial spirit that has gripped His church. It is time to confront the spirit of apathy. Radical Christianity has taken a back seat for far too long. As believers, we have become increasingly ashamed of what we are supposed to be—authentic disciples of Jesus.

A desire has stirred in my heart for the church to become aggressive and passionate again. This is what God created us to be, and He wants to restore to us that quality of life that has been lost. It's a sold-out position toward Him that we cannot forfeit.

Undoubtedly, He wants to ignite that fire within us. The call to unshakeable passion has been made. The search is on for radical people. While talking to a dear friend about Christians that are so intense in their faith that even fellow believers think they're crazy, he said, "This is supposed to be normal Christianity." The only reason their dedication is so shocking is because the bride of Christ has become so cold in her heart. May we endeavor to drive ourselves beyond what is considered *normal*.

In a time when much of the Christian world has become apathetic, the unsaved world is not apathetic at all. They are very vocal and passionate about their beliefs. While the world is confident in what they believe, the church has not exhibited that same type of passion for the things of God. May we challenge that, and see God's people awakened in an irreversible way.

Reclaim the lost art of discipleship. Recapture stolen passion, and regain the lost ground in your life. Future generations are depending on our obedience—don't delay. Plan B is no longer worth looking at. Stoke the flame of revival, torch all alternatives, and run with God.

AFTERWORD

An Exhortation to Men

IN 1968, PHILLIP Morris, a cigarette and tobacco manufacturing company, teamed up with the Leo Burnett agency and began an ad campaign targeting women for their new line of cigarettes called Virginia Slims. The slogan, "You've come a long way, baby," expressed the progress women had made up to that point.

Today, women have indeed come further and achieved much in almost every area imaginable. However, as women have progressed, many men have not. In fact, women are more likely to attend church faithfully and serve in ministry than men. Statistically, women read their Bibles at higher rates than men. Call a special prayer meeting, and don't be surprised if the women outnumber the men.

I know some Holy Ghost-filled women, and their lives are an inspiration. As a man in ministry, I do feel urged to ask, where are our men? My desire is to see fire stirred in the hearts of men and for fresh vision to be caught.

Prove Yourself A Man

> "Now the days of David drew near that he should die, and he charged Solomon, his son, saying: "I go the way of all the earth; be strong, therefore, and prove yourself a man. And keep the charge of the LORD your God: to walk in His ways, to keep His statutes, His commandments, His judgments, and His testimonies, as it is written in the Law of Moses, that you may prosper in all that you do and wherever you turn..." (1 Kings 2:1-3 NKJV)

Just one man in the Bible carried the title, "Man after God's own heart," and that was David. Here he was on his deathbed, giving his last words to his son, Solomon. A man speaking on his deathbed is going to say the most important things he has learned in life, especially to his son, his own flesh and blood. Mixed within the instruction was a charge that separates the boys from the men; a line that throws down the gauntlet. That phrase is, "prove yourself a man." The same charge that David gave Solomon is the charge that God is giving us as men.

Proving yourself to be a man looks less like riding a Harley and yelling at the TV and more like humble servanthood and vulnerability. The fact is, men face insecurities on a regular basis and being able to face those down and overcome them is, in large part, the proof of manhood.

A man of God does not run from the challenge or the truth. He does not quit every time things go upside down. Instead, men of God dig their heels in and continue forward. The question is begged, though, what does that look like? Does it mean we just grit our teeth and silently press ahead alone? *No.* Men of God let other men help them. Yes, this runs against ego and pride, but those things never did anything good for you anyway. The reason I dedicated an entire chapter to impartation is because impartation and vulnerability go hand in hand. It's true that when the going gets tough, the tough get going—but where do the tough get going to? The biblical mandate is that our knees hit the floor in prayer and worship. The scriptural solution is that we crack open the Bible and seek out words from Heaven. God's idea of "the tough get going" is that we open our hearts to other men of God in our lives and allow them to lock arms in our fight.

During one of our church leadership meetings, my wife said that she was encouraged when the women in the church started opening up to her and allowing her to speak into their lives. She said she could see a radical change in them for the better. She complimented the women, and she suggested that the men need to do the same thing.

Right then, I said, "Hold on. Most men won't open up or be vulnerable with me because they know I'm going to tell them what they don't want to hear. Also it seems like when I begin to speak into the lives of some men, according to God's Word, and it goes against their flesh, they walk away complaining, and some even get mad at me for being their pastor."

The truth is, I am not supposed to say what men want to hear but rather what the Word of God says. My job description can include rebukes and chastisements, not to put pampers on men. Have you seen soldiers in Basic Training? Certainly, the military trainees do not tell their drill sergeant that they are being too hard on them. Yet for some reason we have tried to sidestep being challenged by spiritual leaders. When we avoid being challenged and take on everything ourselves, we also avoid being *encouraged*. Not all pastoral counseling is a bunch of browbeating. When you close yourself off, you also forfeit much needed, life-giving words of affirmation and comfort.

This vulnerable, open approach to struggle will make you immune to giving up. I've seen men lose out because they tried to fight alone and caved. Depression, for instance, is an issue that men like to deal with privately. The fact is, there are times when God places a key to your physical, mental, or spiritual health in the heart of someone else, and the only way to unlock those doors is to open yourself to another person. We are not a source within ourselves. Instead, we are interconnected in a global network called the church of Jesus, and God has designed the system to keep us plugged in. This not only takes vulnerability, but it takes discipline. Progressing in faith or in life without discipline is a pipe dream.

We, as men, can complain about not having enough time to pray or read our Bibles, or we could go to bed earlier, get up earlier, and carve out time for it. Do you lack the discipline to do so? Have someone call you in the morning and keep that routine until it becomes your own. God is asking us to show initiative. This is not a sprint, so start with small steps.

Keeping Your Word

There was a day when a man's word was his bond. A handshake between two men alone meant more than a room full of attorneys and legal contracts. Business is rarely done via handshake today, and integrity has been eroding more and more. Keeping your word is not just a solid idea, but an absolute constant must for anyone who calls themselves a Christian.

The Bible describes a righteous person as one "who keeps an oath even when it hurts" (Psalm 15:4 NIV). There have been times where keeping my word has cost me money. Once I promised in my heart to do something for one of my pastors, and some other people did not follow through with their commitment, but I gave my word and it wound up costing me thousands of dollars. Nobody knew, not even the pastor himself. But, I made a covenant with God. He had told me to do something, and even if everyone else bailed, I was not going to violate my integrity with Him.

Beyond money, keeping my word has also cost me lots of time. I want to finish what I start. I want to be a man of integrity and not an inactive leader who begins big projects but never follows through. I do not want to carry the reputation of being a rebel, a quitter—someone else can have that. As a leader in your home, in your church, and over your own life, be someone who does not waiver after making a commitment. Unfaithfulness can cause us to not want to finish what we started. Ask God to help you be faithful in all areas of life. There are desires in all of us to make a difference in the world. When we get saved and discipled in good churches we want to make a difference and change the world. Yet, after a while, we can take a back seat and become inconsistent. Our call is to daily devotion. Jesus requested "daily bread," not "occasional treats."

This is the day-in, day-out lifestyle of a Christian man. Our lives are to be dominated by the simple integrity that God prescribes in His Word. We live in a time where guys would rather get a prophecy or have somebody lay hands on them. If they fall out in the spirit and wiggle like a fish on the ground, then it means God touched them. As great as all that may be, at the end of the day *character* is not transmitted in an impartation at the altar. It's built by people who continually kill their flesh and build the nature of God in themselves.

Read the Bible, find out God's direction for your life, and stand on His promises and principles. It will be harder than it sounds, but the alternative is genuine destruction. All those who claim to be men of God must hold onto the Word of God without excuses. Regardless of anything, the Bible counsels us to do everything as unto the Lord. That alone will mark a shift in our attitudes and our responses towards others. From that posture, God will always have our *yes*.

The truth is, God honors this sort of faith. Without faith, pleasing God is an impossibility (see Hebrews 11:6).

Men of God prioritize their lives around the Word of God and lead their homes with faith. Their children are able to see them submit to the Word of God at home. Their wives see them submit to church leaders and pastors who speak the Word of God over them. If a man wants to harm his family, bellyaching about leadership is a sure way to do it. I've watched it happen, and I too have been guilty of these attitudes at times.

On many occasions, failure to be Christlike on a man's part has left the wife feeling tired of fighting, and sometimes she refuses to keep going. Then when the husband is ready to get things right the wife is no longer interested. It's too little, too late. Obviously, God can swing miracles in any marriage, but the fact is, when men lead like they are called to from the start, you prevent much headache and heartache. Being consistently stable is a more desirable miracle than being pulled out of an all-out crisis.

A man who proves himself to be a man will be the best husband, the best father, and the best worker in the kingdom of God. This is a man who takes responsibility and does not blame shift. This is a man who humbly admits fault and puts in the work to correct the course. God is challenging His sons, to do something and to not just sit there. Take action.

Remember, we referred earlier to the passage, *"From the days of John the Baptist until now the Kingdom of Heaven suffers violence and the violent take it by force"* (Matthew 11:12 NKJV). Advancing the kingdom of God does not come easily because we live in a wicked world full of sin. There is a spiritual battle with our flesh and with an enemy who opposes the will of God. It is going to take a man to *oppose* the opposition of the flesh and the forces of evil.

Made to Conquer

Many men live in a paralyzing fear of failure. If this isn't dealt with, they will never take a step forward. For most, when they fail, they are determined to never even try again. They stop, they quit, and they carry that lump of failure in their throat forever. Sadly, this is what happens with many of us, even if for just a season. Men throw out their young dreams of being the best dad they can be when they realize they messed up in parenting. After failing as a husband, they check out and stop trying altogether.

It happens in leadership too; when things don't go as planned or their shortcomings are on display, they cave. When attempts at achieving success anywhere in life do not pan out, the temptation is to allow past failure to speak louder than the truth of the gospel. Instead of letting your past cripple your future, let your future defy your past. Don't spend your energy trying to eliminate risk and the chance of failure. It's a trivial pursuit. Instead, spend your energy on leaping when God says leap.

As men we are good at putting up a facade and giving a surface-level, "I'm good," when asked how we are. We stand up tall, put on a happy face, walk into church, and blend. Afraid of not measuring up to others, we are weary of standing out and terrified of failure. It seems better to not try than to face the crushing blows and feelings that accompany failure. The fact is, from the start of creation, God has worked with man to put aside past failures and begin *again*.

Abraham, for instance, was called to a land which he did not know. God simply told him to pack up his stuff, get his family, and start walking. He had to fight for his family, and for his heritage as a patriarch. Other men in the Bible had their "unknowns" to enter. Moses, as an example, faced the pharaoh, the most powerful ruler of his day, to free the people of God and with God's help, he led them out of Egypt, a superpower nation, with no conventional weapons or tools except a wooden staff and trust in God.

David fought Goliath with a mere slingshot and five small smooth stones, four of which he did not even need. David did not even fit into the armor he was offered, so he went on without it because he was determined to fight his enemies and the enemies of God. Nehemiah, tasked with building a wall for God, raised up men who had a hammer in one hand and a sword in the other, ready to build and ready to fight simultaneously. The nature of these men, through and through, was to conquer. All of them had their issues, their defeats, and their pasts. Oscar Wilde said, "Every saint has a past, and every sinner has a future." They were not perfect men, but they pressed into the calling of God despite their issues.

What do our kids need from us? All of the possessions we never had growing up on demand? Of course not. They need us to be men of God. Our wives need the same thing from us. Our stance ought to be "as for me and my house we shall serve the Lord." (Joshua 24:15 NKJV). We were saved, not for the purpose of punching a passport to Heaven but to occupy our place as godly men in the earth. Our call has never been to be emasculated men, fearful of the future or our own status. We have been designed by Christ, the Great Architect, to conquer and fight, to live out the dreams and visions God has assigned to us.

Shrinking back is not our response to difficulties. Checking out with a bunch of TV, or addicting ourselves to sports, are not healthy coping mechanisms. May we lead our families into the things of God, and not to selfish, vain pursuits. Above money and ambition, our first pursuit is the kingdom of God and His righteousness. Without this, our priority system will be out of whack. Our quiet times with God were not meant to be dominated by distractions and noise. As men, we are called to overcome the enemy, and to do this, we must make time for undistracted prayer and Word.

Men that do their best to take the Word of God seriously do not gather just for food and fellowship. While those things are great, the truth is, great men gather because of the Bible. It's the magnet of the assembly. Its message has touched and forever altered their lives, rescuing them from a path of destruction and hell. No doubt, the path was going to destroy them, their families, and their future. Someway, somehow, the Word of God came to their lives, and as they read it for what it is, they were challenged and changed. From then on, church is no longer a nice hangout but an immersion into the very Word that changed everything for them.

This is manhood.

Consider yourself. How are you doing with the command to be a man of God? Have you proven yourself to be a man? Or proven yourself to be something else? To prove is to demonstrate—to express something through speech and lifestyle. We know that the world is passionate about what they believe and demonstrate it regularly—and I personally wonder if our faith is demonstrable in our lives as well? The church suffers when men have lost their tenacity. Be a hardworking fighter like our forefathers. Don't cave and cling to a soft, cowardly version of manhood.

Upside Down

Some years ago, I spent a month in California during the holidays. It was my first time doing so in 16 years. My wife, son, and I went into a store in downtown Los Angeles where we saw a guy wearing make-up and high-heeled pumps. He was a big and rough man walking around with a boyfriend. The opportunity presented itself, so I began to share the gospel with him.

His response?

He tried to kiss me. Naturally, we walked away and got in the car. To be honest, my heart went out to him. Somewhere along the way, he had lost what it meant to be a man. On the flip side, we see the same inversion with women. Never in my life have I seen more women act and dress like men. These are the last days where genders are changing, and it has not caught God and His Word off guard. The Bible prophesied that days like today would come when people call good evil and evil good (Isaiah 5:20). Men are losing their identity, in part, because of a lack of leadership. Maybe they grew up without a good dad to impart spiritual truth. Perhaps they have been abandoned or hurt by men who should have protected them. Regardless, the remedy all comes down to men submitting themselves to Jesus and setting a godly example.

When I got saved in 1987, the church was chock full of men who wanted to be discipled. In fact, there were more men at a men's meeting than women at a women's gathering. Men outnumbered women during outreaches and prayer meetings. The usual statistic had been flipped in that church at the time. Obviously spiritual commitment is not a competition between the two genders, but the trend of male apathy in church is troubling. I long to see men take their place and find greater involvement in the house of God, with less fidelity to their personal agendas. Men ought to live fired-up lives, with intense passion. These men don't have to be resurrected every week in order to live for God. They are focused, disciplined, and they thrive anywhere you place them.

Their priority is simple: serve the Heavenly Father and not be dependent on outside pursuits. Strong in faith, they are not shaken by trials nor swayed by how much money they have or do not have. Such men have made a solid decision for God and that decision is not up for grabs.

They are men who are not afraid to stand in the kingdom, battle-ready, bravely facing obstacles that arise. They are committed to God, their family, and the ministry God has placed in their life. They are loyal, with good character, and willing to sacrifice. They help the hurting, protect the vulnerable, and keep their word.

Hopefully, this describes you. If not, our great example found in the life of Jesus is ready to be emulated. It's been said before and is worth repeating, going to church does not make you a Christian. Attending a men's discipleship meeting does not make you a disciple. Having a cross on your shirt does not make you a man of God. The lazy, apathetic, and spiritually dry view of manhood has to be turned upside down. When our definition of manhood is turned upside down, we will turn the world itself upside down (see Acts 17:6).

Historically, we can point with pride to the men of old who have lived lives of genuine manhood, whether it's Paul laying down his life, Martin Luther withstanding pressure and starting the Reformation, or Wesley who challenged men to champion the gospel to the ends of the earth. We have no shortage of examples, but perhaps we have a shortage of men willing to follow those examples.

We need men who will be able to stand by their deathbed like Apostle Paul, and say words like, "I have fought the good fight, I have finished the race, I have kept the faith" (2 Timothy 4:7 NKJV). May the confident words of Paul be ours as well one day. I hope they say that about me and about you. This is the very thing we are fighting for. All adventures have risks, and no doubt we are probably going to get beat up once in a while—that's life. Challenges will likely scare us, but *that* is the time we have to look at the Scriptures and decide whether we are going to prove ourselves to be men of God or not. The difficulties of life are the proving ground of manhood.

Most of us, if we are to be honest, spend a great deal of our prayer time asking God to make life easier. When does it ever occur to us that God wants us to fight? Instead of asking God to fix our marriages, give us prosperity, straighten out our kids, and take away our problems, what if we began asking Him, "Lord, what are You trying to teach me? What do I need to sacrifice? What issues in my heart should I deal with? Would You help me to depend on Your grace as I fight the good fight?"

I have discovered, though, that sex and prayer are similar. So many men talk about it but very few do it. To attempt the Christian life without fervent prayer is spiritual suicide. Begin setting the tone of your household through fiery prayer, worship, and time in the Word. Men of God dictate the tone of our culture. We dictate the tone of revival. The answer to real revival is not somewhere out there in the clouds—it's in you. There are people coming up behind us who will follow in our tracks. So what path are we carving out? Let's hold up the banner of God in our generation for the example of future generations. Biblical manhood is not a flimsy concept on paper. It is a demonstrable reality for you to take on and live out. We could prove ourselves to be men, or prove ourselves to be something else. If our lives are speaking loudly—and they are—my question is: what are those around you hearing?

PASTOR KELLY LOHRKE and his wife, Esther, began The Cure Church on September 11th, 1993. They were sent from California, having never been to Kansas City, but trusting God throughout their journey. Fast forward thirty years, starting with just a small group of eleven people, they have successfully birthed a thriving network of churches across the nation. What sets these churches apart is that they were planted by individuals who were birthed from within The Cure Church itself, including their pastors.

For more information, visit:
THECURE.CHURCH

www.ingramcontent.com/pod-product-compliance
Lightning Source LLC
Chambersburg PA
CBHW011353160426
42811CB00113B/2354/J